1001 little parenting miracles

1001 little parenting miracles

Esme Floyd

CARLTON
BOOKS

THIS IS A CARLTON BOOK

Text and design copyright © 2008
Carlton Books Limited
Illustrations copyright © Carol Morley

This edition published in 2008 by
Carlton Books Limited
20 Mortimer Street
London W1T 3JW

A CIP catalogue record for this book is available
from the British Library.

ISBN: 978 1 84442 837 3

Printed and bound in Dubai

Executive Editor: Lisa Dyer
Senior Art Editor: Anna Pow
Design: Ed Pickford
Copy Editor: Clare Hubbard
Illustrator: Carol Morley
Production: Janette Burgin

CONTENTS

INTRODUCTION

Did you know that singing songs will help your baby learn language? Or that a child often has little giveaway 'tells' like sucking in their breath before a tantrum, which can offer you forewarning?

From calming a newborn baby and dealing with toddler tantrums, to fussy eating and teenage angst, this book contains 1001 little gems of information to show you how small changes can make a big difference and to help you get the very best out of family life. The tips are astonishingly easy to follow and focus on bite-sized pieces of advice sourced from a range of experts from around the world. An essential buy for time-starved parents, this book is a one-stop resource for how to deal with all parenting dilemmas.

Top ten little parenting miracles

4
HEALTHY EATING
WHEN PREGNANT
(see Don't Be a Dieter, page 9)

40
HELP YOUR BABY TO SLEEP LONGER
(see Create a 'Night' Feeling, page 17)

79
BREASTFEED WITHOUT
DISCOMFORT
(see Break the Seal, page 26)

145 DON'T FORGET TO PLAN FOR THE FUTURE
(see Make a Will, page 40)

179 TREAT A SORE MOUTH
(see Suck on an Ice Cube, page 50)

442 LET YOUR TODDLER CHOOSE
(see Allow Individuality, page 104)

803 MAKE DIFFICULT SUBJECTS EASY TO DISCUSS
(see Sex, Drugs & Washing Up, page 181)

884 TRAVEL WITH EASE
(see Stroll Around, page 198)

947 THROW A GREAT PARTY
(see Send Siblings Away, page 209)

956 STAY SAFE IN THE SUN
(see Keep Them Covered, page 210)

pregnancy & birth

1 GET THE LATEST ADVICE

If you've had one child already and are pregnant for a second time, make sure you talk to your midwife or doctor about the latest advice. Often, advice for pregnancy and parenting can change from year to year with new research, so make sure you're up to date.

2 TAKE FOLIC ACID

Research suggests that taking 4000 mcg of the B-vitamin folic acid every day from when you start trying to conceive to the twelfth week of pregnancy will help protect your child against neural tube defects such as spina bifida.

3 FILL UP ON FIBRE

Many pregnant women feel constipated. Eat plenty of high-fibre foods such as wholemeal breads, wholegrain cereals, baked beans, fruit and vegetables, to help regulate your movements.

4 DON'T BE A DIETER

When you're pregnant dieting could lead to you depriving your developing baby of nutrients. Choose healthy snacks like fruit, cereal, baked beans on toast or cheese and crackers, and aim for an extra 300 calories a day above your normal intake.

5 RELAX AND ENJOY

It's tempting to spend your pregnancy working as hard as you can to save money, moving house or getting changes made to your existing house. But don't forget to take time to relax and enjoy it – your baby will benefit from the relaxation hormones and you'll feel more prepared for the birth and for looking after a newborn baby.

6 KEEP ACTIVE

Experts suggest giving up contact sports and those that involve lots of impact such as running, horse-riding, skiing, etc, during pregnancy, as they could contribute to miscarriage. Try yoga, cycling, walking and swimming instead.

7 BE A FISH LOVER

Women who eat at least two portions of oily fish per week during pregnancy have been shown to have children who perform better physically and mentally at school age, so eat up those fish suppers or take an omega-3 supplement.

8 GET TOGETHER

Three to four weeks before the birth of your baby is a good time to start getting ready for your new arrival. Involve your partner in choices about furniture, travel systems and so on, and stock up on basics such as nappies, cotton wool, baby wipes and a changing mat.

9 D IS FOR PREGNANCY

If you're pregnant make sure you get enough vitamin D – the substance is manufactured by the body in response to sunlight and it helps the body utilize calcium efficiently, which is essential for strong bones and teeth. Vitamin D can be taken as a supplement – 10 mcg a day.

10 BACK TO BACK

Many women suffer back pain when they are pregnant, especially in the last few months, so begin practising good lifting habits and posture at this stage. After birth, be careful with the way you pick up the baby: try to bend your legs rather than your back, as the ligaments are still loose and prone to damage, and keep your feet facing forward.

11 KEEP UP THE CALCIUM

Pregnant mums may need more calcium because of the huge demands pregnancy puts on the body, and to help the developing child's bones stay strong. Aim for three servings of milk, cheese or yogurt a day.

12 SOOTHE THEM WITH MUSIC

Scientists now believe babies can hear in the womb. Make the most of this by spending 10 minutes a day for the last six weeks of your pregnancy relaxing to the same piece of music. You may then be able to use that music to help calm the baby once it is born.

13 DON'T BEND DOUBLE

During pregnancy – especially in the second and third trimesters – your abdominal muscles are stretched, which means they find contraction difficult. Try not to do too much bending or lifting and steer clear of abdominal exercises such as sit-ups. Never try to lift anything that is awkward or heavier than 9 kg (20 lbs) and avoid lifting heavy objects above the waist

14 BE YOUR OWN JUDGE

When it comes to putting on weight during pregnancy, every woman is different. Don't judge yourself by what happened to your friends or family; be guided by your intuition. Eat sensibly and keep as active as possible.

15 LIVER YOUR TIMBERS

Pregnant women should avoid eating liver and foods containing liver – such as pâté and liver sausages – because they contain high levels of vitamin A which could be harmful to the unborn baby.

16 SAY 'NO' TO NUTS

If you are pregnant and you or the baby's father, or any of your other children, suffer from allergies (including asthma), it is best to avoid peanuts and foods containing peanuts while you are pregnant and breastfeeding.

17 PICTURE A HAPPY PLACE

To help you concentrate on relaxation and breathing during labour, take along a picture of a place or moment at which you remember feeling totally relaxed and happy. As you breathe, try to regain that feeling.

18 AVOID THE BUG

Listeria is a bug that can lead to miscarriage or severe illness in the newborn infant – it is rare, but it's best for pregnant women to avoid pâté, blue cheese, undercooked ready-meals and mould-ripened cheeses.

19 ORDER IT WELL DONE

Toxoplasmosis is a bug that has been shown to cause harm – including blindness – to the unborn baby. Pregnant women should avoid undercooked meats, unpasteurized cheese, unwashed salad, fruit and vegetables, and raw or undercooked shellfish.

20 TAKE YOUR TIME

If you're planning a hospital birth, especially if it's your first baby, don't rush too early to the hospital. Labour is likely to progress better if you are in a place you find comfortable and happy, so stay at home as long as possible. Call your midwife or the hospital when contractions are every 5 minutes and last 30-40 seconds. However, prepare to go in immediately if you are less than 37 weeks, you haven't felt the baby move recently or you aren't coping well.

21 RELAX AND UNWIND

As the time to give birth approaches, try to spend at least 10 minutes a day practising your breathing and relaxation techniques so that when the time comes it will feel like second nature. Research shows that relaxed mothers are less prone to birth complications.

you & your newborn

22 NO SHAKES

You should never shake your baby. It can be incredibly frustrating and upsetting looking after young babies, especially when they cry a lot, but it's better for your baby to let them cry than risk hurting them by shaking.

23 DON'T CRY IT OUT

Most experts agree it's impossible to spoil a young baby with attention – the more they get, the more secure they feel. Respond to their cries for food, changing, holding or soothing and don't worry that you might 'spoil' them at this young age.

24 CRYING FOR NO REASON

Accept that in the first few months your baby will sometimes cry for no reason. Understanding the difference between a 'hungry', 'tired' and 'comfort' cry is helpful, but don't worry if you can't always tell what your baby needs (it might not be anything!).

25 GIVE BABY A HEAD START

A new baby is not strong enough to support its own head, so be sure to avoid injuries by carefully supporting the head and neck when you hold, carry or pick up your baby. Remind family and friends to do the same and show them how if necessary.

26 STAY STILL

You shouldn't exercise for around six weeks after you have given birth, because your body needs this amount of rest time to allow the abdominal muscles to contract and join together again, as well as to tighten the ligaments. Exercising too early could lead to them not fusing properly.

27 KEEP UP THE EXERCISES

Don't forget your kegel exercises during the first ten weeks after you have given birth. Exercising the pelvic floor muscles feels like holding in a pee (although you shouldn't do it while peeing) and you should aim for ten contractions in a row. Do it at a regular time – such as every time you have a drink or after you've been to the loo – so you don't forget.

28 GET SOME REST

Having a baby can be a stressful time – not only are you exhausted from giving birth, there's no chance to catch up on that sleep now your baby's around. Try to get as much rest as possible, talk to family and friends and make sure you eat well.

29 SLEEP WHEN THEY DO

When you first have a baby don't fall into the trap of being so stressed you don't allow yourself to rest. Take the time while they are asleep to rest yourself and catch up on some of that night-time sleep deprivation. Invest in a baby monitor if you're worried you won't wake up when the baby cries.

30 LET THEM HELP

Often grandparents want to be involved from the very first few days of a baby's life, but family time just for the baby and parents is important too. Grandparents may feel more involved if you give them specific jobs that will help you such as cooking meals or helping tidy the house.

31 MAKE THE MOST OF YOUR 'TIME OFF'

If your partner takes the baby off your hands so you can have a break, don't waste it by worrying that they're not doing the right thing. It can be difficult for primary carers to accept that theirs isn't the only way, but as long as you're consistent on rules, anything goes.

32 TAKE YOUR TURN

Why not take alternate days at the weekend for you and your partner to have a lie-in during the morning? Just one longer sleep a week can make a real difference to your tiredness levels and your mental health, so think about taking turns at looking after the kids.

33 DEAL WITH DEPRESSION

Post-natal depression isn't just feeling a bit overwhelmed after the birth of a baby, nor is it the 'baby blues' which hits shortly after birth as your hormone levels plummet and which lasts anywhere from a few hours to a day or two. Instead, it's a genuine mental illness that can last weeks, months or even years. If you feel you might be suffering, seek medical advice and support immediately.

34 SEEK ADVICE

Mothers who have undergone difficult births are more likely to be among the one in ten women who suffer post-natal depression. Speak to your health visitor or general practitioner (GP) or join a support group with other mothers.

35 JOIN A GROUP

Parents and carers of babies and toddlers with special needs may have additional anxieties to those of other parents. Many parents find support groups with parents of other special needs children can be a tremendous help.

sleep like a baby

36 NIGHT AND DAY

Your newborn won't know the difference between night and day. Babies are not born with the ability to sleep through the night so you'll need to be available day or night to begin with and gradually teach the baby the difference.

37 CREATE AN AMBIENCE

By the time your child is three to six months old, they will be able to recognize their surroundings. Make sure you create a restful place for them to drop off to sleep at night, not a room filled with clutter, harsh lighting and bright colours.

38 CALM DOWN

You can't force your baby to sleep, so don't bother trying, Instead, use your energy to create a sleep environment that is relaxing, calming and conducive to dropping off, and reflect this in your behaviour. Your attitude to night-waking will affect your child's sleep habits forever.

39 MAKE SOME NOISE

Music, noise and even specialist 'white noise' tapes can all be good ways to help babies get off to sleep or just calm down, but beware of using the same sleep prop too often as your baby grows up in case they begin to depend on it.

40 CREATE A 'NIGHT' FEELING

When you have a new baby, getting up in the night can be exhausting. New babies are likely to sleep for around two to four hours in one stretch overnight, rising to six hours by the time they are three months old. Start as you mean to go on by making 'night' different from 'day', using soft lights, voices and sounds to encourage your baby to stay sleepy rather than waking up for playtime.

41 BEWARE IF YOU BED-SHARE

You should never share a bed with your baby if anyone in the bed has a sleeping disorder, is a smoker, has been drinking or taking medication that causes drowsiness or is very tired, as this will affect wakefulness.

42 ENCOURAGE SLEEPING

Try to encourage good sleep patterns early on with your newborn by putting the baby down to sleep when nearly asleep, but not quite. The sooner they learn to do that last bit of falling asleep on their own, the easier it will be for everyone.

43 DON'T LEAVE THEM BE

Some research has shown that babies left to cry for long periods when they are very young (in the first few months of life) might stop crying, but their stress levels remain high. Most babies are fine if left for 5, 10 or 15 minutes, but if crying continues they might be becoming stressed.

44 STAY SMOKE FREE

The risk of sudden infant death syndrome (SIDS) or 'cot death' as it is often called, increases if either of a baby's parents smoke or if anyone is allowed to smoke in the same room as the baby. Keep your child away from second-hand smoke and ask smokers to refrain for an hour before they handle your child.

45 KEEP THEM CLOSE

It's a good idea to keep the baby's cot (crib) in your room at night to start with so that you can respond to their cries before a grizzle turns into a full-blown cry and they wake themselves up. This can be important if you have other children, too, so they aren't disturbed.

46 STEER CLEAR OF THE SOFA

Whatever your baby's age, don't fall asleep with them on a sofa, as this can be the cause of accidents and has been shown as a risk for SIDS. It's possible to roll on to your baby or for them to get trapped between your body and the side or back of the sofa or its cushions.

47 CONSIDER THE CONSEQUENCES

While the idea of having your baby sleep in the bed with you might seem like a good idea at times, before you decide to go ahead with it make sure you carefully consider all the consequences for everyone – is it something both you and your partner are comfortable with?

48 LAY THEM FLAT

Don't leave your baby to sleep for long periods of time in a car seat or reclining seat where their backs are bent. Babies' bones are very malleable when they are young, so laying them flat is better for their backs.

49 PLAY FOOTSIE

If you are using covers for your baby rather than a baby sleeping bag, make sure you place them 'foot-to-foot' to sleep – that is, with their feet touching the foot of the cot (crib) – so there is no chance they can wriggle under the covers and suffocate.

50 STAY BACK TO SLEEP

At five to six months, the risk of SIDS drops dramatically and this usually coincides with the baby's ability to turn themselves over, which means they have more control of their movement. Don't worry if they roll over onto their front, but do still put them on their back to sleep.

51 SHUSH!

There is no need to worry about normal household sounds if your baby is asleep at night but you haven't gone to bed, as most babies won't wake up with general background noise. However do be aware that sudden loud noises, such as doorbells, explosions or gunfire on the television or blaring music may waken your sleeping baby.

52 LIE THEM NEARBY

If you like the idea of sleeping with your baby but are worried that you might harm them if they lie in your bed with you, why not put them in a moses basket next to your bed or invest in a special co-sleeper cot (crib) that attaches to the side of the bed?

53 RAISE THE BED

If your baby has a cold it can often cause sleep problems. Try raising one end of their cot (crib) so they are sleeping on a slight slope, which will help clear their nose. But avoid this if your child has weak lungs as it could make any cough worse.

54 CHECK THEIR TEMPERATURE

One of the main worries many parents have is that their baby will get too hot or cold. Keep a room thermometer on the wall near their cot (crib). Don't worry if hands and feet are cold – concentrate on forehead and chest for core temperature.

55 KEEP COOL

Adults know how difficult it is to get to sleep when it's too hot but your baby depends on you to control the night-time temperature. Make sure they're not too hot by choosing appropriate clothes and testing their temperature from time to time.

56 TAKE CARE WITH CO-SLEEPING

The safest place for your baby to sleep is in a cot (crib) in your room. If you do want your baby to sleep in your bed there are many factors you need to look into to ensure that it is going to be safe – for example that the bed is big enough, the mattress firm and that there is a tight fit between the mattress and the bed frame. Research this thoroughly to ensure you have taken every precaution necessary.

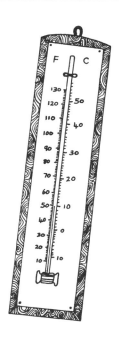

57 SLEEP ENVY

Don't get too envious when your friends tell you that their baby's sleeping through the night at three months – scientists define sleeping through as sleeping for five hours in one stretch in infants under six months (not the whole night).

58 MAKE YOUR OWN RULES

Don't let anyone else tell you what to do when it comes to your family's sleeping arrangements. What works for one family won't work for all, so set your own rules and don't rely on other people's preferences.

calming crying

59 DON'T SHOWER THE SYMPATHY

There's evidence that babies' pain thresholds actually develop as a result of their parent's reactions to falls, cuts and other bumps. To help your child deal with pain as they get older, don't smother them with sympathy they don't need.

60 DON'T JUMP TO ATTENTION

Try to avoid responding to every noise your child makes at night – many children cry while they are sleeping or as a way of getting back to sleep if they wake up. Leave it a few minutes before going to them and don't pick them up straight away; a pat on the back might be sufficient.

61 RESPOND TO DIFFERENT CRIES

Never ignore your child if they wake at night and their cry sounds different to their normal waking pattern. High-pitched, continuous cries and low groaning sounds can often be signs of pain and shouldn't be ignored.

62 MASSAGE AWAY TEARS

Often, babies will cry when they are young because of some gastric discomfort. If it is indigestion or wind, it can often be helped by a gentle abdomen massage (use gentle strokes from their right hip, up to the ribcage and back down to the left hip). Use calming oils like lavender or camomile to boost relaxation (always seek advice from a professional on how to use and what are the appropriate amounts).

63 KEEP HOLD OF THEM

If you have a baby who is prone to crying a lot – or colicky – try holding them. Often, babies respond to being held and will cry when left alone, even if they are somewhere familiar. Using a carrier can help save your arm muscles, particularly around the house.

64
FRESH AIR

For some reason, babies often respond positively to a walk or trip outside. Put them in a baby carrier or pram (baby carriage) and get out into the fresh air for 10 minutes or more – the change of scenery will often stop crying and grumbling in its tracks.

65 CHOW DOWN

If your baby is crying because of teething pain, try letting them chew on something cold (like a teething ring), which will ease pain and swelling. If this doesn't work, use distraction and try teething gel (although avoid putting this too near to the back of their throat as it could numb their tongue).

66 SWADDLE TO SOOTHE

Many babies respond well to being swaddled when they are very young. Wrap a blanket firmly (but not too tightly) around them, holding arms and legs secure. Some babies fight to free themselves – in this case, a half-swaddle – leaving the arms free – often works.

67 WARM THINGS UP A BIT

If your baby seems uncomfortable and won't stop crying, try putting their blanket in the tumble-drier for a few minutes or draping it over a radiator (being careful of fire risk) to warm it up before you snuggle them into it.

breast & bottle feeding

68 LATCH THEM ON

Getting your baby latched on to breastfeed for the first time can be hard for some women. When a baby is feeding correctly, most of the brown aureole around the nipple is in their mouth and it shouldn't be painful.

69 EAT UP FOR FEEDING

If you're breastfeeding, you will probably be hungrier and thirstier than usual. Make sure you drink lots of water and eat lots of good quality foods to keep your milk quality high – breastfeeding isn't the time to be thinking about dieting.

70 DITCH THE COFFEE

Some experts believe traces of substances such as caffeine can be found in breastmilk, so it's best for breastfeeding women to avoid drinking too much caffeine, avoiding it completely in the hour before a feed in case it upsets the baby.

71 FREEZE YOUR MILK

Even if you're breastfeeding, your partner can help share the burden of those round-the-clock feeds if you express your milk. It will keep for 24 hours in the refrigerator or a month in the freezer, and the baby can then be fed by bottle. If you're freezing the milk, make sure you label the container clearly with the date on which it was expressed and frozen.

72 STAY UPRIGHT

If your baby is unusually fussy after feeding they may be suffering from gastro-oesophageal reflux (GER), which can also cause pain when lying down. Try holding your baby upright for at least half an hour after feeding, and prop them at a slight angle to sleep.

73 FOSTER THEIR APPETITE

Don't worry if your baby suddenly feeds all the time and it feels like your breasts don't have enough milk. Allow them to feed until they're empty as this is a way of them 'ordering' larger portions. Often, it takes a day or two for you to catch up with your baby's growing needs.

74 KEEP A LOG

It's a good idea to keep a log of breast-feeding times for the first few months of feeding your baby. This way you will be able to see patterns emerging and can adjust your feeding schedule appropriately. It's also useful when you're talking to medical professionals.

75 LET THEM FEED

A lot of the anxiety around breastfeeding is about not being able to see how much the baby is drinking. If your baby's putting on weight, has wet nappies (diapers) several times a day, and doesn't have signs of dehydration like dry lips or a sunken fontanelle, they're getting enough.

76 OFFER SECOND HELPINGS

If your baby is bottle-fed and they drain their bottle completely, offer them more in case they're still hungry. Never change the powder to water ratio of the milk, which can affect digestion; simply make a little bit more so you can be sure your baby is filling up.

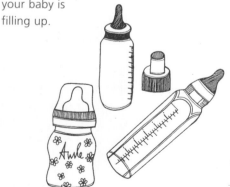

77 SHARE THE LOAD

If you are bottle-feeding, share the responsibility. Your partner could give some of the night feeds or do the last feed before bed so that you can have an early night and catch up on some sleep.

78 DON'T BLITZ THE BOTTLE

Microwave ovens heat liquids unevenly, and can leave super-heated pockets of formula in your baby's bottle. Even if you vigorously shake the bottle afterwards, heating bottles in the microwave should be avoided.

79 BREAK THE SEAL

When your baby has finished feeding, don't try to pull your nipple straight out of their mouth, which could be very painful. Instead, carefully insert your finger in the side of their mouth to break the seal before moving them.

80 PROP UP THEIR HEAD

If you're breastfeeding lying down at night (or following a Caesarean) and your baby is having difficulty, prop them to a 30-degree angle. This will help them to drink and swallow the milk more easily.

81 BOTTLE THE IRON

Most experts advocate breastfeeding as the best kick-start for your baby's health. If you choose not to or can't breastfeed, make sure you choose a formula that's fortified with iron to keep their levels high.

82 REMIND YOURSELF

Many nursing bras now come with a 'reminder' system so you can remember which breast you last fed from and keep the alternate feeding schedule. You can make your own with a safety pin or ribbon!

83 STICK TO MILK

Until your baby is four to six months old they shouldn't need anything except milk, so avoid giving them water or juice until they start eating protein in the form of solid foods. If they seem thirsty, offer them breast or bottle.

84 WATER BABY

Water is the best alternative drink to milk. For babies less than six months old use tap water, but boil it first and let it cool to make sure it's free of any bacteria. Avoid bottled water as it can have higher mineral and sodium contents.

85 MAKE TINY MOVEMENTS

Many babies feed a lot more calmly at night and swallow less air, meaning they need less burping. Try to keep movements as small and calm as possible at night to avoid waking them up too much and if you do need to burp them, soothe them at the same time.

86 WATER IT DOWN

Citrus fruit juices can be used after six months. They're a good source of vitamin C, but are acidic and have a high sugar content, so dilute with water. Squashes, fizzy drinks, flavoured milk and juice drinks are unsuitable for babies as they contain sugars.

starting solids

87 LET THEM GET USED TO IT

Remember your baby will never have felt anything but milk in their mouth until you give them their first solid feed. If it looks like they're spitting it out, don't assume they don't like it. It might just be them exploring the new sensation on their tongue.

88 GET THEM HUNGRY

When you're introducing solid food to your baby, choose a time when they are usually especially hungry (for lots of babies this is first thing in the morning or lunchtime rather than the evening) and introduce their first solid foods at that meal.

89 WAIT A WHILE

If your baby is strongly resistant to solid food the first few times you offer it and becomes upset or really spits it out, wait a week and try again with something else. By then they'll have forgotten about the previous experience.

90 DON'T RUSH IT

Don't expect your child to manage more than a few spoonfuls of food once or twice a day to begin with, and don't worry if there's less in their mouth than on the floor! You're introducing the entire concept of eating, so don't rush it.

91 KEEP IT COOL

Remember that young babies are really susceptible to burns from hot food. Make sure you always test the temperature of food before serving and be extra careful of hot spots if you use a microwave.

92 START THINGS BLANDLY

It's a good idea to start your baby off on really bland foods like baby rice, then progress to puréed vegetables (like carrot and sweet potato), and then stewed and puréed fruit. It's best to use organic produce. Introduce one fruit or vegetable at a time so you can watch for any tastes they don't like and also for allergic reactions.

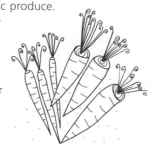

93 VEGGIES ARE GOOD

For vegetable first foods, choose produce that is as fresh as possible, wash it well, cook until very tender and then purée thoroughly with a blender, food processor or food grinder/mill, adding a little boiled, filtered water or milk to ensure a smooth, lump-free consistency.

94 MAKE THE TRANSFER

If you're freezing your baby's foods in ice cube trays, as soon as they are frozen, transfer the cubes to ziplock bags to keep them as airtight as possible. That way, they will keep longer without crystallizing. Cooked vegetables keep for two months in the freezer.

95 WARM THEM WELL

To defrost and warm frozen cubes of vegetables and fruit, place cubes in a heat-proof dish and warm in a pan of simmering water. If you use a microwave, leave for a minute and stir well after heating to avoid hot spots. Never reheat uneaten food – throw it away.

96 ICE HOT MEALS

If you've heated up your baby's food too much but they're screaming with hunger and you don't think they can wait any longer, try stirring an ice cube into it to cool it down as fast as possible. Most meals will absorb the extra water without it affecting the taste and texture of the dish.

97 LET THEM DRINK WATER

It's a good idea to offer water with meals to get your baby used to eating and drinking together, but once they can hold their own cup it might be necessary to limit the amount they drink to prevent filling up on water.

98 DON'T FORCE THE ISSUE

A good sign that your baby has had enough to eat is if they turn their head away from the food and purse their mouth shut. If they do this and don't respond to gentle persuasion, don't force them to eat any more.

99 SPOON CLEVER

If you're worried about burning your baby by feeding them food that's too hot, consider investing in a heat-sensitive spoon that changes colour if the food is too hot. Similar gadgets exist for testing the bathwater, too.

100 COOK UP SOME FRUIT

When you're first introducing fruits to your baby, it's best to peel and cook them slightly (except banana) before feeding, as they are absorbed better that way. Apples and other fruit with thick skins are best peeled for a smoother purée.

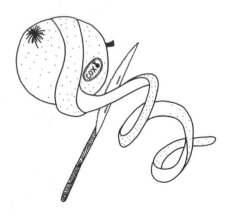

101 NO ADDED SALT

Don't add salt to your baby's foods (or to the water if you're cooking vegetables) and try to avoid adding sugar, as both of these substances can put undue pressure on your baby's still-developing liver. Choose natural products.

102 CUT DOWN THE MILK

Once your child has accepted solid foods as part of their routine, cut down their milk feeds and increase solid feeds gradually so that they are getting more and more of their calories from solid food.

103 GET STEAMY

For baby's first meals, steaming is preferable to boiling because valuable nutrients can be lost in the water of boiled vegetables. A good idea is to steam in batches and freeze purées in ice cube trays, then simply defrost when needed.

104 ONE AT A TIME

Try to introduce one food at a time and wait a few days before introducing another new variety. This will give you the chance to monitor your baby for any signs of allergic reaction.

105 SIT UP AND EAT

It's best to start feeding your baby with them sitting up in a high chair or in a supportive seat rather than leaning back. This will help them develop the right musculature for eating at a table later on and reduce the risk of choking.

106 STAY AWAY FROM EGGS

Fresh eggs are an inexpensive source of high quality protein, but they have been known to be allergy-producing in infants, especially the whites. It is generally recommended that infants not be introduced to egg white until after 12 months, although the yolk can usually be safely offered at around 10 months.

107 DON'T OVERFILL

Babies will gag if too much food is placed in their mouths, and once they start feeding themselves, this is likely to be a regular occurrence. Unfortunately, gagging also often leads to vomiting. Try not to worry; offer food again and help them regulate their portions.

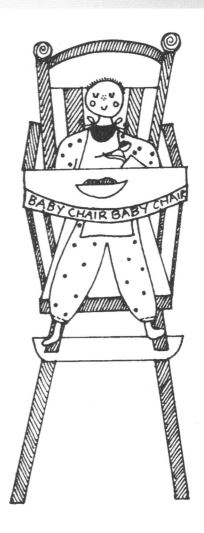

108 CUT OUT THE CITRUS

Citrus fruits such as orange and grapefruit and those containing acidic juices like pineapple, mango, strawberries and raspberries are best left until after your baby is a year old, to avoid stomach upsets. If you feed them before, try not to do it more than a couple of times a week.

109 TRY AND TRY AGAIN

If your baby refuses to eat a new food, don't force the issue. Try offering the food again a day or two later, and remember that experts say a baby doesn't officially 'not like' something until they've refused it around ten times.

110 MOVE IT ON

Just as it's important to make sure first foods are well puréed, it's essential to move on to the next stage as soon as your baby is ready. Move from puréed foods to mashed and then to lumpy and finger foods to help them develop the muscles needed for chewing. This will also help speech development.

111 HOLDING THEIR OWN

Well before your baby is old enough to start feeding themselves, it's a good idea to let them hold a spoon. Even if they just wave it around, it will get them used to making the link between feeding themselves and eating.

112 FILL UP ON FINGER FOODS

Usually between the age of seven to eight months, your baby will show signs that they want to feed themselves and are therefore ready for finger foods. To minimize choking risk, foods should be soft such as cooked carrots, peas and sweet potato or banana, avocado and melon.

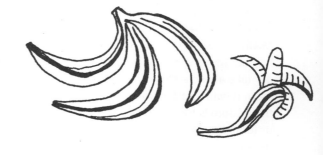

113 SPOONFEED THEM

Don't use a bottle for feeding solid food, even if the lack of mess seems tempting. Part of the reason for feeding solids is to learn the difference between eating and drinking, so starting off by making this distinction will make it easier later on. Use a set of cutlery specifically designed for babies as they will be the correct size and more gentle for the mouth.

114 PULSE YOUR PROTEINS

At about nine months, pulses such as beans and lentils may be introduced. These are very nutritious and contain protein so are a great choice for vegetarians. Start out with small well-cooked servings and don't feed more than twice a week to avoid wind.

115 MASH UP A MINI MEAL

For 'out and about' fresh meals on the go, take a whole banana or avocado and mash it with a fork into a smooth pulp. If the mixture is too thick, add a little breast- or formula milk. Organic fruits are best because they are chemical-free.

116 CUT DOWN ON MILK

If your baby has a cold, allergies or simply seems to be producing more phlegm than normal, try cutting down on their intake of dairy products, which have been shown to increase mucus production in some children. Use soya or rice milk instead.

117 KNOW YOUR HISTORY

Be proactive about allergies – know your family history and that of your partner regarding food allergies and intolerances. This will help you look for patterns if your baby starts showing signs of intolerance such as rashes, hives and bloating.

118 PLUMP UP THE PROTEIN

Babies are ready for protein at around seven to eight months. Start with white fish and bland meats such as chicken to get your baby's system used to protein, before moving on to beef, lamb and oily fish like salmon and trout. Meat alternatives such as puréed or mashed beans and lentils may also be offered. These provide the iron, protein and energy needed for growth.

119 BLITZ YOUR MINCE

Even though mince (ground meat) seems almost mashed as soon as it's cooked, it's a texture that many babies find difficult to eat. Once cooked, blitz the meat for a minute or so in a food processor to turn it into a smooth paste.

120 STEER CLEAR OF HONEY

Honey might seem like a harmless way to sweeten foods, but avoid using it before your child is one year old because it contains a risk of botulism, which could cause them to become ill and could cause an upset stomach.

as your baby grows

121 STAY ALERT

Remember that even if your baby couldn't roll over last night, they might be able to this morning. Make sure you never make assumptions about what they can and can't do and never leave them unattended.

122 MAKE IT PUBLIC

The period before your child can crawl and walk but after they're big enough to realize there's a world out there can be frustrating for everyone. Make the most of it by taking them to restaurants, libraries and other public places where they can see lots going on around them.

123 PLUG THE PLUGS

Once your toddler understands how to run the taps in the bath, it's a good idea to remove plugs from their reach. Not only will this stop them causing a flood, it could also prevent drowning if they filled up the bath and fell in.

124 BE A LESS CLEAN FREAK

Experts now actually believe that keeping your child's environment too clean could lead to autoimmune problems such as asthma and hay fever as they grow up. Exposing them to a range of bugs and bacteria seems to boost immunity, so don't be too worried the next time they pick something up off the floor and eat it (so long as it's food!).

125 GET AN ALL-IN-ONE

Everyday all-in-one 'babygrow' clothing and underclothes will help to keep your baby's tummy from being exposed and will keep them warm and comfortable. You can also get waterproof all-in-one suits that will protect them and their clothes from water and mud. You won't need to avoid taking your baby outside because of bad weather when they start crawling – the suit will let them enjoy the rain.

126 HAVE A GAME OF PEEKABOO

Play peepo with your baby as you pull their T-shirt or jumper over their head. Getting them to enjoy dressing their top half early will pay dividends later when they'll be begging to do it themselves rather than fighting it.

127 TAKE OUT A TOY

To keep them happy in their pram or pushchair (baby carriage or stroller), take along some of their favourite toys if you go for a walk or on a journey. Attach toys and books to the sides of the pram so they've got something to look at, touch and play with.

35

128 A COT BREAK

Putting the baby in a cot (crib) or play-pen with some toys to play with is a great way for you to grab 5 minutes to make a phone call or do another essential job. Try not to do this when you're angry or if they're upset, as the child may begin to associate playing alone with bad feelings.

129 BOUNCE AROUND

Many babies really enjoy door bouncers and they can help strengthen leg muscles and boost core strength. However, make sure you don't overuse them, which could cause your baby problems in the long run. Up to 15 minutes once or twice a day is best.

130 VANISHING ACT

Separation anxiety is something most children go through – usually at nine months and in some children reappearing around 18 months. Make sure you never vanish when they're not looking; always tell them where you're going and make sure they aren't left with people they don't know.

131 KEEP THEM TRIM

Once you're baby's nails have hardened a little you'll need to cut them to stop them from scratching themselves. Use baby nail clippers and perhaps enlist someone to help you. This job is easier with two! Because a baby's fingers are so small to start with, some parents gently nibble the end of the nail off. Steer clear of scissors.

132 HANG A MOBILE

To help your child stay still and calm on the changing table, think about reserving a few toys especially for changing time; alternatively hang an interesting mobile above their changing mat to distract them from the job in hand. When buying a mobile, choose one that allows you to vary the elements hanging on it so your baby has something new to look at.

133 TEETHING PROBLEMS

Teething can cause many physical problems – runny stools, dribbling, rashes and a slightly raised temperature as well as increased crankiness – but it shouldn't cause illness, vomiting or high temperatures. If you're worried, see your doctor.

134 DON'T RAISE A CANNIBAL

It's tempting to let your baby chew your fingers when they first start teething, but bear in mind that teeth will become more plentiful and sharper in no time. It's best to offer non-human alternatives to avoid biting problems later!

playing & development

135 JOIN A LIBRARY

Why not join a toy library if there's one in your area? Children often play with toys exhaustively and then lose interest for a few weeks or months. Joining a toy library can help save money and give them a great variety of things to play with.

136 WATCH YOUR LANGUAGE

Your baby will understand much of what you are saying long before they have the language to communicate back to you. Remember this when you are talking about their behaviour and be aware of what they might overhear.

137 DON'T DISAPPEAR

When your children first start to play with other children, they will need adult intervention to help them learn to share and take turns. Once you've set up the game, leave them to it but don't disappear – hover around to help if problems arise.

138 SING ALOUD

Babies often respond brilliantly to music and singing, but did you know that it's hearing real voices rather than tapes that is most beneficial to their development? Lose those inhibitions and get singing.

139 SING A STORY

Songs and stories are an important part of language. Not only do they help children learn the rhythm of words, they also teach about rhyme and – because they are repetitive – children can learn them over time, which helps teach anticipation.

140 START A CONVERSATION

Teach your baby the art of conversation by taking turns with them to make sounds. Even if they're still at the 'ooh, aah' stage, it's important to let them see you interacting in response to the sounds they make.

141 LIMIT THEIR TOYS

Small children do need toys to play with, but don't fall into the trap of buying them everything in the shop. A few toys they can really explore are better than too much choice, which may limit their concentration.

practical parenting

142 KEEP A TRAVEL PACK

If you drive around to visit places a lot, it's worth using the glove compartment of your car to keep a few nappies (diapers), some nappy bags and some wipes in case you get caught short or run out on your next trip.

143 DO A DREAM FEED

Many experts suggest waking your baby for a feed just as you go to bed so the two of you can enjoy a longer stretch of sleep. The period between this 'sleepy' feed and the next is often their longest stretch of sleep.

144 ENOUGH TO EAT

If your baby suddenly begins to wake up again at night at around six months old for feeds, make sure you're giving them enough during the day. As babies get busier, they often forget about being hungry. Timetable feeds so you tank up your child in the daytime.

145 MAKE A WILL

If you and your partner aren't married but have had a child, it's essential you make a will protect your child, as in many countries unmarried partners don't automatically inherit from each other. In many countries, if the mother dies and the parents aren't married, the father may not automatically become the child's legal guardian.

146 GET A GUARDIAN

If you're a single parent, divorced or separated, it's vital you include in your will a nominated guardian for your children, especially if there have been issues with parental rights and responsibilities in the past.

147 RING THE CHANGES

Over the course of their life your baby will require somewhere in the region of 5,000 nappy (diaper) changes. Make it easy on yourself – and your back – by putting their changing mat on a table at a comfortable level where you don't have to bend down.

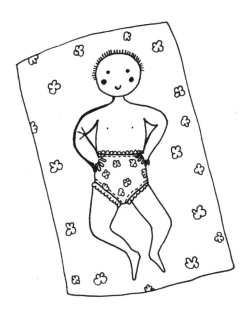

148 SETTLE THE FUTURE

Once you've settled in with your baby, it's worth thinking about some practicalities – if something happened to you or your partner, who would take care of your child? Make a will and appoint executors to help your child handle their finances, and think about who they would live with.

149 CHANGE BEFORE FEEDING

At night, think about changing your baby's nappy (diaper) before a feed even if your usual routine is to do it afterwards. Changing it beforehand will mean they can fall asleep straight after feeding, which you probably want to encourage.

150 VISIT THE DENTIST

It's never too early to get a professional to look at your child's teeth. Get them used to visiting the dentist early and you won't have so many problems later. Ask your dentist for advice on age-appropriate dental hygiene – many recommend that a child should visit a dentist when the first tooth comes in.

raising a little angel

151 GIVE THEM A KISS

When you praise your child, reinforce it with physical behaviour too. Children love affection, so as well as saying 'well done', hugging, kissing, scooping them up and even rough and tumble or tickling are all considered 'treats'.

152 THE RIGHT TIMING

It's important to use rewards at the right time so there can be no possible confusion about why your child is being rewarded. Only reward behaviours you want to increase but make sure you reward them every time they happen.

153 BE SINCERE

Don't ever give false praise to a child. Even as young as 18 months, children can understand the difference between achieving something and not. Look for things to praise but don't be false – they'll start to lose trust.

154 BE CLEAR HEADED

Make sure your children know exactly what you expect from them. For instance, 'when I call you, I expect you to stop what you are doing immediately and come to me'. But once you've set the rules, don't abuse your position – only call them if you have to and praise them when they come.

155 READJUST YOUR BODY CLOCK

Toddlers don't know the meaning of the word 'patience' – which means you've got to have it in spades if you're going to get along with them. Accept that it takes years to learn urgency, and try to readjust your body clock to toddler time, at least for the time being.

156 PRAISE BE!

Don't forget the best reward for your child is often simply your praise and delight at something they've done well. Don't fall into the trap of not responding to good behaviour – remember to say things like 'thank you for tidying your toys so well' and 'you did a great job coming downstairs when I called'. Positive feedback reinforces good behaviour.

157 TALK ABOUT TIMESCALES

Remember to talk to your child not just about what they are doing at that moment, but what they have done and what they are about to do. Toddlers begin to grasp the concept of time at around the age of two, so giving them the language to express themselves helps them to develop. Point to a clock too, so that they begin to connect activities and time.

158 BECOME A COMMENTATOR

One of the best ways for toddlers to learn about language is to hear you commentating on what they're doing. It might feel like you're talking all day, but your chattering will pay dividends for your child's language skills.

159 LEARN THE ROPES

Toddlers will be too young to understand a 'timetable' of their daily routine, but talking to them about it will help it stick in their mind. As they get older, you can ask them questions – 'we've had supper and tidied up, what happens now?'

160 LISTEN WELL

Toddlers are often frustrated by trying to communicate things to you that you don't understand. Even if the words they are saying are beyond you, give signals that will let them know you are trying to understand such as eye contact, tilting your head to one side and nodding.

161 HOW WOULD YOU FEEL?

Find a willing friend or partner and hold a brief conversation with while they stand and you kneel on the floor. You may find yourself feeling uncomfortable listening and speaking to someone who's towering over you. This is how your child feels, so get down to their height to make the most of your communication.

162 USE YOUR WORDS

Toddlers don't understand that their actions have an effect on other people. Try to explain things to them using simple words – 'let's share the toy with Suzie because that will make her happy', or 'you mustn't hit George because it will hurt him and he'll be upset'.

163 AN EVEN KEEL IS BEST

We all know consistency is important, but it really is important to good behaviour. Don't fall into the trap of changing your behaviour according to how good/strong/tired/stressed you feel on any given day. It's often easier to stick to fewer rules, so try to avoid too many 'nos'.

164 BE POLITE

Most parents want their children to be polite and use words like 'please' and 'thank you', but if children don't hear them in use regularly, they are unlikely to ever use them themselves. Make an effort to be polite in front of your children and they are more likely to behave well themselves.

165 TALK ABOUT FEELINGS

Promote empathy in your toddler by talking to them about stories you have read or films they have watched. For instance, if you've been reading Cinderella, talk to your child about how upset she was because her stepsisters were mean to her.

166 KNOW YOUR NOS

Once your child nears the age of two, their favourite word will become 'no'. It's not that they really mean it, it's just that they're learning that they have some control over their world. If you find it hard to deal with, try cutting out 'yes' or 'no' questions and ask things like, 'would you like yogurt or strawberries?' instead of 'would you like a dessert?'

167 CONSISTENCY IS KEY

It's important that your child gets consistent rules on behaviour from all their carers. Make sure grandparents, nannies and other carers know your major behaviour rules and how you enforce them, and choose a nursery that reflects your beliefs.

168 GIVE THEM THINGS THEY CAN DO

Frustration is a big part of toddler's lives – they know what they want to do, but invariably they can't quite do it yet. Help your child by giving them toys and jobs they can manage, and helping them with those they find difficult. Simple tasks like cleaning up can give them confidence in their skills.

169 DEAL WITH DEPRESSION

Even little children get depressed. If your toddler doesn't seem happy or is acting differently, try and find out what is upsetting them. If nothing seems to work, check with your health visitor or doctor, both of whom might be able give you advice.

170 HAVE FUN!

Keeping a positive attitude and concentrating on the fun side of your toddler's life can lift your spirits, even when you're feeling down. Make an effort to join in their play and find time to laugh together. Enjoy activities with them whenever possible – whether at the playground, in your garden or in front of the TV.

incidents & accidents

171 NEVER HOME ALONE

Never leave babies or young children at home alone, sleeping or awake, not even for a few minutes. There might be all sorts of danger you're not aware of. Make sure you plan trips around wake times, take them with you or get a sitter.

172 CHECK REFERENCES

When it comes to leaving your baby or children with others, follow your instincts. If you have any doubts about a childminder, babysitter or other carer, don't take them on. Always ask for at least two references and check these carefully.

173 FOOLS RUSH IN

If your toddler falls over, don't immediately rush to their side to offer comfort. They're close to the ground to start with so can often fall or trip without being hurt. Wait until they cry or call out before you worry.

174 GO DOWN BACKWARDS

Once your baby starts to crawl, begin to show them how to turn around and descend the stairs on their knees backwards. If they know how to get down before they try to work it out for themselves, you can hope to avoid them trying to slither down on their front, which could be dangerous. You should, of course, be right behind them with your hands at the ready, every step of the way.

175 COMFORT THE BUMP

As they begin to understand the limits of their body, small children can feel hurt emotionally by small bumps and bruises that don't bother them physically. Don't dismiss their feelings; by responding to their worries you are teaching them you understand how they feel.

176 DON'T REACT TO REACTION

It can be really draining when you feel your child is overreacting to something you think they should be able to take in their stride, but remember they're still learning about emotions. Instead of telling them they shouldn't feel a certain way, listen.

177 FENCE OFF WATER FEATURES

If you have a swimming pool or pond in your garden, make sure it is either fenced off or covered in safety netting to avoid your toddler getting themselves into dangerous situations. Make sure fences and boundaries are secure if neighbours have open water.

178 MAKE BATHTIME FUN

If your toddler becomes resistant to spending time in the bath (or is frightened by the taps (faucets) or plug, which is also common) try to make bathtime extra fun with bathtime mirrors, games and songs. Let them choose a new bath toy and play with bubbles and containers to pass the time.

179 SUCK ON AN ICE CUBE

If your child burns the inside of their mouth by eating food that's too hot or taking something from your plate or cup, help them heal quicker by giving them an ice cube to suck. The cold will reduce the swelling and pain.

taming tantrums

180 KEEP YOUR COOL

Never respond to a toddler tantrum with anger. Not only might this frighten the child when they are already emotionally charged, it will teach them that tantrums elicit a reaction. Try to keep your cool no matter how hot you're feeling.

181 CAUSE A DISTRACTION

It's a lot easier to stop a tantrum that's just starting than one in full bloom. With young children, distraction often works. As soon as you see the tantrum starting, get them interested in a toy or a game. Even being silly or tickling them sometimes works.

182 TAPE YOUR TANTRUMS

If your child's tantrums are getting on top of you, set up a camera in the room and record both you and your child's behaviour. Watch the tape back with your child and talk to them about what you both could have done differently.

183 BREATHE IT OUT

Some toddlers hold their breath when they have a tantrum. If your toddler does this, take a deep breath yourself and don't worry. Breath holding is almost always a harmless phase. However, some children can hold their breath until they pass out, which can be a very frightening experience. Do seek advice from a health professional if this is the case.

184 A CUDDLE CAN CALM

It might be the last thing you want to do to your screaming little monster, but a cuddle can sometimes calm your child if you scoop them up and soothe them. Be calm and kind and assure them you understand their frustration.

185 DON'T GIVE IN

A lucky few parents will get away without tantrums, but most will suffer. The number one rule is not to give in to it to keep them happy or quiet – if a tantrum works once, it will be longer the next time, and it's harder to break a behaviour pattern than to stop it emerging in the first place.

186 SECURE THE AREA

Many children have very physical tantrums, flinging themselves around and flailing their arms and legs. If your child does this, make sure they can't hurt themselves, other people or damage objects. It might be necessary to pick them up and move them out of danger's way.

187 PUT WORDS IN THEIR MOUTH

If you think your child is frustrated at not being able to explain how they feel and might be about to explode, try helping them by saying things like, 'maybe you're angry because you can't have that toy?' If they agree, explain it's OK to be angry, but it's not OK to lose control.

188 LEAVE THEM TO IT

As long as your child can't hurt themselves or anyone else with their tantrum, consider stepping back, giving them some space and leaving them to it. They may soon stop if they're not getting any attention. If there's a crowd of interested onlookers, however, or you're embarrassed, you may have to take them somewhere quiet.

189 READ THE SIGNS

Most children have give-away signs, like sucking in their breath or making a hand gesture, that signal they might be about to erupt. Once you've learned your child's 'tells', you can head off the tantrum before it occurs.

190 TALK IT THROUGH

Often, children react with angry, tantrum-like behaviour when they're experiencing emotions they can't explain. Try talking to your child (during a calm playtime, not while they're mid-scream) about how they feel, helping them link words and feelings.

191 CALM IT DOWN

Tantrums are more likely if your child is stressed, hungry or tired. Try to minimize stressful activities, carry healthy snacks and don't over-plan your toddler's day, which could lead to them not being able to cope.

feeding time

192 TOOLS FOR THE JOB

Let your toddler use a cup, fork and spoon as soon as they can. It might be frustrating for you to see their food land on the floor yet again, but they'll feel more independent and meals will be less of an issue.

193 LET THEM DECIDE

It's understandable that parents worry about feeding their babies and children – food and nutrition is vital for their health and development, and it's your job to get it right. But try and allow them to set the boundaries rather than you – it's their body, after all!

184 NO ALTERNATIVES

If your toddler refuses to eat more than a few mouthfuls of their meal, don't clear it away and offer them treats or snacks instead. It's important for them to learn that if they don't eat what you put in front of them, nothing else is on offer, otherwise they're likely to do the same at every meal.

185 BRING ON A BUFFET

If toddlers have their friends over for a playdate, create a finger food buffet of healthy snacks such as apple moons, banana wheels and cheese bricks, or provide different shapes of fruit, vegetables, cheese and egg and invite them to make their own food pictures.

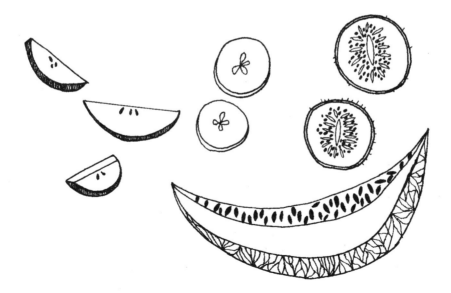

186 KEEP IT HEALTHY

Children might be born with a naturally sweet tooth, but they're not born craving sugar and junk foods. Try to start as you mean to go on by introducing a range of natural, healthy flavours from an early age and keeping junk foods to a minimum.

187 KEEP THEM WHOLE

Children should drink whole milk until they are at least two years old because they need the extra calories. After two, they can gradually move to semi-skimmed (low-fat) as long as they are eating well the rest of the time.

188 MAKE IT YOURSELF

Research suggests that children who have eaten homemade rather than pre-prepared foods as youngsters are more likely to eat a varied diet – including vegetables – as they get older, probably because they are used to different flavours. Try and give them homemade whenever possible.

199 PICK UP A PAN

Processed foods provide a high proportion of the saturated fat and salt in our diets, so one of the most effective things you can do for your whole family's health is to start making your own meals. It doesn't have to be complicated – pasta with tomato sauce is a great healthy choice.

200 KEEP SERVINGS SIMPLE

Offer your child food that is tasty and looks good, and offer the right amount. A good rule of thumb is to offer 1 tablespoon of each kind of food for each year of your child's life. If your child is still hungry, you can serve more.

201 CHOOSE ORGANIC

Once your child reaches the age of one, they can start drinking cow's milk instead of formula. There is evidence to suggest that organic milk is higher in omega-3 oils, vitamins A and E and other antioxidants, so choose organic when you can.

202 GIVE HEALTHY SNACKS

If your child doesn't eat at one mealtime, offer a nutritious snack such as fresh fruit, vegetables or cheese and crackers a few hours later. Even if they don't eat the snack, they will usually eat at the next meal. With this approach, you can be sure your child won't have a poor diet.

203 MEASURE BY THE WEEK

Don't worry if they don't eat much in one day. Chart their food intake over a week before you worry they aren't getting enough nutrients. Toddlers need between 1,000 and 3,000 calories a day but they don't need to eat this amount EVERY day.

204 OBEY THEIR STOMACHS

Teach your child a valuable life lesson by not forcing them to clean their plate. Allowing them to stop eating when they feel that they have had just enough will help them maintain healthy eating patterns in adult life.

205 DIP AND DUNK IT

Toddlers love dunking pieces of fruit, vegetable or breadstick into anything... it's almost as much fun for them as painting, with much the same result on their bib and the tabletop! Try fruit with yogurt or vegetables with hummus or sour cream.

206 TAKE ADVANTAGE OF HUNGER

A great way to get your toddler to try new foods is to introduce them when you know they are hungry or at snack time. Trying them at the end of a meal might encourage them to refuse if they are already nearly full.

207 ATTACK THE SNACK

Try to balance your child's request for a snack with the family's need to enjoy a regular meal together. If the meal is several hours away, you can offer a bigger snack such as a piece of cheese or a banana, but if the meal's in the next hour, make it smaller and explain why.

209 MINI MARVELS

Try to work with your child's preferences when it comes to how their food is served, to make them feel more comfortable. Some prefer small plates, cups and spoons, whereas others prefer to struggle with the adult versions.

210 AVOID ALLERGENS

Avoid substances that are known to cause allergic reactions – like nuts, shellfish and eggs – until your baby is a year old, or three if you or your partner suffer a nut allergy. After this, you can introduce them slowly but be vigilant in looking for reactions. Symptoms usually show up within minutes to two hours following ingestion.

208 B SURE ABOUT VITAMINS

Growing children should have a vitamin-rich diet if you want to keep them in tiptop health. Vitamin B complex is essential for growth and development, and one of the best sources is yogurt, so aim for at least four servings a week.

211 TAKE A TEST

If there's a history of allergy in your family and you're worried that your child might have inherited it, talk to your doctor about running a few simple allergy tests, which can give you peace of mind. But beware – some allergies don't show up until the child is around three.

212 HIDE THEIR VEG

If your attempts to 'hide' vegetables in bolognese, soups and stews have failed because your toddler has super keen eyes, try puréeing them before you stir them in – most toddlers won't pick out the taste without the texture.

213 BIN THE BRIBES

Try not to bribe or force your child to eat. Threats or punishments aren't a good idea either. If your child doesn't want to eat, accept their refusal. Even though you may be concerned, don't show your child that you are upset as they may try to gain your attention in the same way another time. When they get hungry enough, they'll eat.

214 DON'T MAKE A MEAL OF IT

When your child is a toddler, their desire to express themselves won't stop just because it's a mealtime. Try to avoid confrontation, distract rather than argue, and avoid conflict situations by, for instance, keeping pudding hidden until it's time.

215 MAKE SOME MOONS

If you're finding it difficult to get your toddler to eat, distract them with a 'moon-making' competition, where you take turns taking bites of their food to see who can make the best moon-shaped bite.

learning to play

216 DON'T TOY WITH TOYS

Many parents automatically decide for their children which toys they can play with, but studies show that children learn best and enjoy play more when they decide how they want to play and at what pace. This also boosts concentration, enjoyment levels and good behaviour.

217 KEEP THE PRAISE COMING

Make sure you praise your child EVERY time they play well with other children to reinforce their good behaviour, and you can start this habit when they are still early in toddlerhood. It's never too early to learn good manners.

218 TIDY UP TIME

In order not to face battles about tidying up when they are older, encourage your toddler to take responsibility for tidying away their toys from an early age. Having a 'tidy time' after dinner or after bathtime can help.

219 DON'T BE A DIRECTOR

When your child is young, try to avoid directing them too much. It can be really frustrating to watch a child doing the same thing over and over again, but you can use description to help you let them lead – for instance, say 'you're picking up the car' instead of 'let's put the car on the table'.

220 ATTEND TO YOUR CHILD

Some parents have a way of being with their children that encourages good behaviour. Psychologists call it 'attending' and it means being aware of your child's good behaviour without leading them into other behaviours. Examples are descriptive phrases like, 'you're putting the ball in the bucket' and 'you're colouring in the rainbow', rather than suggestions or questions.

221 FIND AN OBSERVER

To make sure you're getting the most out of play, enlist the help of a friend or relative. Get them to watch you playing with your child and take notes. Who instigates the play? What behaviour is encouraged? And so on. Discuss the results and work out ways you can develop further, keeping it FUN.

222 ASK PERMISSION

Instead of rushing in to join your child when they are playing, show some respect by asking them if they'd mind if you joined in, or what they'd like you to do to help with the game. That way, you're priming them to ask before interrupting.

223 MAKE A PLAY PLAN

Could you be limiting your child's play with your own constraints? Ask yourself questions: Do I enjoy playing with my child? How often do I play and for how long? What are the barriers that can get in the way and how can these be gradually removed? Make a plan that will help you enjoy play more.

224 BRING OUT A BALL

Keep a ball in the pushchair (stroller) and in your car so you can start up an impromptu game if you get caught short or plans change. Likewise, packing a few books will mean your child has on-the-spot activities to occupy themselves.

225 GO OFF-PAGE

Don't feel you have to stick to the story when you're reading to your child. As they get older, children might want to impose their own stories and rich imagination on the book. You can help them develop their imagination by asking questions such as, 'what do you think happens next?' or 'why do you think that happened?'

226 SEE IT EYE TO EYE

When you play with your child, make sure you get down to their level, have eye contact and show them you're interested. If your child is sitting on the floor, sit down there with them so that you're part of the game rather than an observer. They will treat you like another child.

227 DO IT DAILY

Reading is a great way to boost your child's language skills as it introduces words they might not otherwise hear or use. Make time for reading every day, even if it's only a few minutes.

228 DON'T PUSH THE BOOKS

Most parents are keen for their children to enjoy books, but be careful not to push them too hard – a lot of children will switch off if they feel they are being made to do something. Let them enjoy books in their own way and their own time.

naughty naughty

229 DON'T PAY ATTENTION

Until the age of two, children find it difficult to distinguish between negative and positive attention, which means that even attention you think is negative – shouting, telling off and so on – can be rewarding to them. Try not to give too much attention of any sort to behaviours you don't want to encourage.

230 PUT YOURSELF IN THEIR POSITION

Put yourself in your child's shoes when it comes to discipline. For whom would you do the best work? The boss you trust and admire or the one you fear? Be fair and calm and set consistent boundaries and your child will respond appropriately.

231 PUNCH A PILLOW

If your child kicks, hits or bites in anger or frustration at not being able to express their feelings, try giving them a suitable outlet instead, like a pillow, soft toy or bed. If they use the alternative, make sure you give them lots of praise.

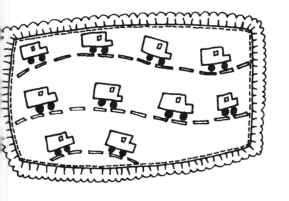

232 SPEND SOME MELLOW TIME

If your toddler is constantly exhibiting very physical behaviour, such as banging toys, bashing things and pounding on walls, it may be that they are struggling to control tension. Encourage and reward gentle behaviour and spend time being mellow with them.

233 DON'T PASS IT ON

Aggression is contagious. Toddlers and young children can pick up aggressive behaviour from older siblings. Dealing with aggression quickly and calmly – and not exhibiting it yourself – will help everyone learn to live more harmoniously.

234 WANT IT, GRAB IT

Grabbing is common in toddlers and pre-schoolers. Explain why they can't have the item they grabbed, ask them to hand it back to the other child or give it to you and offer a replacement. Make sure you're not modelling the behaviour by snatching off them.

235 GET A GENTLE TOUCH

Toddlers don't understand how much they can hurt someone if they hit them, and this goes for people, dogs, cats, babies and anything else. Instead of scolding them, show them how to be gentle and give lots of encouragement.

236 POWER IT DOWN

Some children bite or push as a show of power. If your child does this, don't reward them by letting them see the other child crying or by picking them up and talking closely to them. Instead, let them know what they did was wrong, remove them from the scene and concentrate on the other child.

237 NO REWARDS FOR BITING

Many toddlers will bite other children – through frustration, anger or simply not understanding the boundaries. Make sure you don't reinforce this behaviour with attention – immediately tell them it's wrong, but concentrate on the bitten child and talk to your child later about why biting isn't allowed.

238 PLAN YOUR REACTIONS

Plan ahead of time what you will do and how you will react if your child hits or pushes someone, so you aren't tempted to react with aggression if you're put on the spot. Giving yourself a plan will help you to remain in control.

239 DON'T BITE THE BITER

Children under three simply don't have the mental tools to understand the consequences their actions have on others. Don't be tempted to 'teach them' by biting, kicking or hitting them if they do it to another child – instead, use appropriate punishment and talk to them about why it's not acceptable.

240 STOP THE VIOLENCE

Aggressive biting and hitting is most common between the ages of 18 and 30 months, when the child doesn't have the verbal language to communicate. Biting usually stops as the child's verbal skills grow, but hitting may not, so make sure you are consistent.

241 SAY YOU'RE SORRY

Usually, by two years of age a child can make the connection between being aggressive and the consequences. Encourage your child to say sorry to whoever they've hurt and even give a kiss or hug if both of them are comfortable with that. They can also bring them a blanket or something that will help soothe the hurt they caused.

242 SAY 'NO' TO HITTING

Remember that your child will learn from you not only about how not to hit, but how to react if someone hits them. If you let them hit you, they might let others hit them. Teach them how to react by calmly but firmly saying 'no' to being hit by another child.

243 FORGET EXPECTATIONS

Don't expect your toddler to behave the same way every day – teething, illness, tiredness, growth spurts and all manner of other issues can leave them feeling grumpier than normal. Try and go with what they need and the difficult phases should soon pass.

244 DON'T TAKE SIDES

When toddlers fight or disagree it's often difficult to ascertain who was the aggressor. Make sure your child gets the message that some behaviour is never appropriate – like biting – but they can take action to protect themselves if attacked.

245 DISTRACT AND DELAY

Before the age of around two, children may find it difficult to understand why they can't do what they want. Instead of getting into a battle, distract them with a toy, observation or song – it will make everyone's life much more pleasant!

around the house

246 WORK AND PLAY

Young children don't distinguish between 'work' and 'play' the way adults do. To them, anything can be a game and they can have great fun helping you, even with jobs you find tedious like sweeping, vacuuming, dusting and washing-up.

247 CREATE A MINI CLOTHES-LINE

Let your child help you with chores such as hanging out the washing by creating their own mini clothes-line and letting them hang some of your underwear or light items. Handling the pegs will help their fine motor skills and they'll enjoy being able to copy you.

248 TIMETABLE YOUR CHORES

If you find your chores and jobs around the home continually get in the way of spending time with your child, try creating a timetable for yourself so you keep playtime and chore time separate during the day. That way, your child will understand the boundaries better.

249 ESTABLISH HOUSE RULES

Make simple rules for your child and be consistent. Start with a few things you do and don't do so they don't become overwhelmed with rules and regulations. Cut the 'don'ts' down to as few as possible and discuss them with your child.

250 DON'T BE TEMPTING

Toddlers are obsessed with what's happening at an adult level and no wonder – they spend much of their life not being able to see! So try to minimize temptation by keeping trailing cords out of reach, turning pan handles inwards and not leaving knives and other sharp objects on the edge of surfaces.

251 DISTRACT TO PROTECT

Next time your child pulls something off a shelf onto their head, drops their food on the floor or any manner of other irritating things, remember they don't realize it's wrong yet. Don't try and discipline them until they're older, just use a firm 'no' and explain why, then distract them with something else.

252 CLAMP DOWN ON CLIMBING

Many toddlers love to climb, but they have no ability to think forward about how they'll get down, or understanding that falling might hurt them. Try to keep climbing opportunities to a minimum and don't keep tempting things – like toys or sweets – on high shelves.

253 MAKE IT SAFE

Once your toddler can walk, it's time to think about safeguarding their bedroom from accidents. Bookcases and chests of drawers should be fixed to the wall wherever possible, plugs removed from basins, windows locked and electrical sockets covered.

254 KEEP YOUR EYES OPEN

Toddlers often make large developmental leaps in just a few days, which means you've got to be extra vigilant when it comes to home safety. That bleach bottle top they couldn't open a few days ago might now be within their capability, so make sure you don't make too many assumptions.

255 DRAWER OF THEIR OWN

If you're going to be spending a lot of time in the kitchen, your child will want to as well. Why not give them their own drawer filled with 'safe' kitchen toys like saucepans, wooden spoons and plastic dishes. Let them play with children's scales and 'cook' while you do.

256 A NON-SLIP BOTTOM

Toddlers who have fallen over in the bath are more likely to be frightened of water and it could be dangerous too, so make sure you invest in a non-slip bathmat, especially if your child is going to be standing up to use the shower.

257 DON'T BE A MUCKY PUP

Avoid leaving a messy playroom for months without tidying it up. Ask your children to help you if they're old enough. Allowing them to get used to living in mess will encourage messy habits as they get older.

258 ROTATE AND REUSE

Keeping to a toy rotation system will help you keep your house tidy because it will stop your child having all their toys out at once and spreading them all over your floors. Encourage your child to help you tidy up when it's time to put the toys away.

258 A GROUP BATH

If your child is frightened of bathing, making it a group event can help turn fear into fun and assuage any anxieties they have. Parents can get into the bath with their children, or simply bathe siblings together.

260 PROTECT THEIR EYES

When you're bathing your baby or toddler, if you're using soap or shampoo make sure you keep a damp, clean flannel or washcloth on hand so you can use it immediately if eyes get splashed.

avoiding problems

261 BUY THINGS IN MINIATURE

Imagine how frustrating it is to live in a house where nothing is the right size for you. Try to include your toddler in the house by buying child-sized tables and chairs or getting a set of steps so they can see onto surfaces.

262 CHOOSE PLAYMATES CAREFULLY

As your child gets older, they will choose their own playmates but until the age of around three the decision is usually down to the parents. Think about which children your child has most fun with and try to see them, even if they're not your favourites.

263 BE PREPARED

If you have no choice but to take your toddler to a school meeting or somewhere where they're going to have to stay still for a long period, make sure they are well-rested, well-fed and have had lots of attention from you earlier in the day.

264 DO A TOY CHECK

If your child is having friends over, make sure you remove toys that could cause problems – both physically, like tennis rackets and anything they could hurt each other with, and emotionally, by making sure favourite items are put away.

265 CHANGE YOUR DAY

It's easier to change your day around a bit than to try to change the temperament of your toddler. Shuffle your schedule to fit their daily mood swings and make the most of energetic times, and you'll all have more fun.

266 ROLE-PLAY TO UNDERSTAND

A good idea to help your children understand if favourite pets have to stay at the vet's or pass away, is to make a pretend vet's surgery for some of their soft toys. Let them lead the play so you can help them address their worries.

267 NOISE SENSITIVITY

Around the age of one year to 18 months, children may develop a fear of loud noises such as dogs barking, the vacuum cleaner and loud bangs. If your child suffers from this, make sure you don't surprise them with noises without warning them first.

woof

out & about

268 GET FAST FOOD

The best restaurants to eat in with your toddler are those that can serve you food fast. Italians restaurants are often good for this as pizzas and pasta cook so quickly, likewise Chinese and other Oriental eateries are good choices. The attitude of staff is a critical factor.

269 BOOK AN EARLY TABLE

If your toddler is used to eating at a certain time in the evening and you're taking them out for dinner, make sure you hit the restaurant half an hour earlier to avoid the hunger meltdown, especially if you may have to wait.

270 MINIMIZE WAITING TIME

Try to minimize the amount of time your child spends sitting at the table before your food arrives. Most toddlers have a sitting still limit of about 15 minutes, so let them run around, take along some toys or take them for a walk beforehand to keep them occupied.

271 TAKE ALONG A CUP

Remember that most restaurants do not provide sippy or spout cups for children, or even straws, so unless your toddler is adept at using a cup without tipping the contents all over their clothes, it's advisable to take a suitable cup with you.

272 AVOID HANGING AROUND

If you're having appetizers and a main course, make sure you ask the restaurant to bring your child's food at the same time as your appetizers to avoid them having to hang around and get too hungry. It will make your experience more enjoyable, too.

273 SPREAD SOME ENJOYMENT

Waste some time at the dinner table while you wait for your food to arrive by allowing your toddler to practise spreading – for instance, butter on bread, peanut butter on crackers or cream cheese on biscuits.

274 STICK TO THE FAVOURITES

When your toddler is still young, and particularly if they are a fussy eater, stick to favourites in restaurants rather than asking them to try new foods – there will already be enough excitement. Older children and good eaters might enjoy trying new flavours, however.

developing together

275 GIVE YOURSELF A TREAT

Don't get sucked into being a martyr for your family. Reward yourself for all your hard work by giving yourself a treat once a month. Simply going to a friend's house, the cinema or getting a manicure is a great treat.

276 TRY THE TOOTH FAIRY

If you find it difficult to get your child to clean their teeth, use the tooth fairy as motivation. If your child thinks they'll get less money (or if you're feeling really strict, none at all) for 'bad' teeth, they're more likely to brush properly.

277 EARLY STORIES

Many parents feel silly or nervous reading aloud to their child. Starting early is a great way to get you both used to sharing some time together. Even as early as a few weeks old, children can respond to their parent telling a story.

278 BECOME A LIBRARIAN

Try to create a home library that is as varied as possible for your toddler, as many of the words they pick up will come from books. Choose stories about people, animals, machines and anything else you can think of to broaden their perspective.

279 BE A CHATTERBOX

The first five years of a child's life are the prime time for learning to talk, and most of your child's language will come from the adults around them. The more time you spend talking to your child, the more you enable them to develop their own language skills. Remember to give lots of praise.

280 EXPLAIN YOUR EMOTIONS

Don't just teach your child 'label' words like 'cat', 'teddy', 'television', 'cookie, 'cup' and so on. It's also important that they learn words that will help them express their feelings, like 'happy' and 'sad'. Lead by example by expressing your own emotions – 'it was a bit scary', or 'I was worried because' are good examples.

281 IT'S ONLY NATURAL

Don't label your child as 'destructive' unless they really are. Toddlers will break, tear, chew, draw on, dribble on (and possibly pee or poo on if given the chance) pretty much everything as part of natural development. Destructive is when older children break or damage things deliberately.

282 LOOK AT YOURSELF

If your toddler uses bad language or is aggressive, think about where they have learned the behaviour. If they're at home with you, look at your own behaviour to see if they are picking up bad habits, and talk to carers as well. Make sure you are setting good examples about positivity too – if they hear you complaining all the time they are bound to pick up some tips.

283 NAME YOURSELF

It can be confusing for very young children learning to talk to hear lots of non-specific words like 'you' and 'me' in sentences. While your child is very young, try to use names instead, like 'Mummy will find Laura's shoes'.

284 LEARN THE HIDING PLACE

Help your toddler learn useful words with a hiding game. Hide something (a toy, ball, cookie, etc) in a room and use words like 'up', 'down', 'under', 'over', 'big', 'high', 'low' and 'small'. Then let them do the same for you.

285 LET THEM LEARN

It's easy to forget – in the melee of housework, getting to places on time and all manner of other jobs – that childhood is about growing up. Try to help your children learn to grow and develop (and if that means sometimes being late because they want to examine an ant crawling up a wall, so be it!).

286 OPEN BOOK

Books are a great way to get your child to talk about their feelings. If they are frightened of dogs, for instance, reading books about dogs might encourage them to open up to you and talk about their fears and worries.

287 BOOKS RIGHT

If your child finds it difficult to concentrate on storybooks, choose picture books with large, brightly coloured pictures and few words. Or make your own books with photographs of familiar objects and people to help them to engage.

288 DON'T SCRAP THE SCRIBBLES

Your child's first pictures will be scribbled masses rather than works of art but don't dismiss them. Talk to them about what they've drawn or coloured in, never laugh or mock and show them you value their efforts by displaying them or giving them to friends and family.

289 COUNT ON COUNTING

Try to encourage your child to count and use numbers every day. Even if it's things like counting the steps to a door or cookies on a plate, every little bit of practise will help your child gain those all-important number skills.

290 DON'T BE SHY

If your child is developing shyness (where they are not simply less confident around strangers, which is normal, but actually seem to exhibit some fear), try to be understanding but not make a fuss. Let them know what to expect from situations so they're not surprised. Be supportive, don't push them and check that you're not exhibiting the same kind of behaviour.

291 POP UP A PUPPET

Help your child to develop their language skills using hand puppets. Instead of starting with complicated stories, try using the puppets to re-enact what your child has done that day, such as eating breakfast or going to the park.

292 TRY SOME MAKE-BELIEVE

Making up stories is a great way to help your child develop language and understanding. Help them 'own' the story by asking them open-ended questions rather than those that can be answered with 'yes' or 'no'.

293 THINK INSIDE THE BOX

It's never too early to start enjoying make-believe. Create a story box containing wooden animals, clothes and hats, building blocks and other toys, which can be used for making up stories.

a good night's sleep

294 FOLLOW THE ROUTINE

If you're taking turns with your partner or another carer in putting your child to bed, make sure you are all following the same routines and stages. Presenting a consistent front will enable your child to better follow the routine.

295 TIRED AND EMOTIONAL

Look for signs your child is getting tired before bedtime when you set your evening schedule – lying on the floor, rubbing eyes, yawning and sucking thumbs or fingers indicate they are ready for bed. Getting upset or fractious can also be signs your child is overtired.

296 KEEP TO BEDTIMES

Set appropriate bedtimes for your child and don't let them creep later and later – having a fairly strict schedule is better for your child and will give you some well-deserved quality time to spend with your partner in the evening. Make sure the bedroom is an inviting and tidy place to go to sleep.

297 SLEEP IS FOR THE BEDROOM

Don't let your child fall asleep on the sofa or chair downstairs and then move them into their bed. This is OK once in a while, but they shouldn't be allowed to get used to it as it's important they learn to go off to sleep on their own.

298 BATH-TIME BLISS

A bath is a great thing to include in your child's bedtime routine, especially if they tend to be resistant to sleep. Bathing causes the body's temperature to drop afterwards, a physical feature that is associated with tiredness, so your child is more likely to feel sleepy.

299 DON'T REWARD WAKING

During the second half of your child's second year (that is 18 months to 2 years) they can be prone to sleep problems and night-waking even if they have slept through well before. If you don't allow them to get up or 'reward' them for waking, this phase should pass fairly quickly.

300 WIND THEM DOWN

Giving your child enough time to wind down before bedtime will help them to learn how to get themselves to sleep more easily, helping you not only at bedtime but also if they wake up during the night. Avoid loud noises, cartoons and games and opt for books and soft music instead.

301 SMALL COMFORTS

It can help your toddler to get themselves off to sleep if you put them to bed with a soft toy, blanket or even a muslin cloth, so they can learn to comfort themselves. Let them choose their comforter rather than trying to force one on them.

302 LIMIT COT/BED TOYS

Instead of putting your child to bed with lots of toys in their bed or cot, which might tempt them to play instead of sleeping, let them drift off with a few soft toys or comforters. You can always put some toys in with them later, then if they wake up early they'll have something to play with.

303 NIGHT-TIME TRAP

If your child wakes in the night persistently over several days or weeks and isn't ill, make sure they know they should be staying in bed at night. Avoid making waking up comfortable by offering attention, food or entertainment, which could encourage them to want to stay up.

304 DOUBLE UP THE DUMMIES

If your child has a dummy (pacifier) at night but wakes up if they lose it and cries until you replace it, why not scatter several around their cot/bed as they go to sleep? That way, they're less likely to lose them.

305 PRIORITIZE SLEEPING

The main issue with solving your child's sleep problems is that it will take time, effort and lots of energy from you. Don't enrol on a sleep training programme or start one at home while you've got other major things going on in your life unless you can make it your top priority – it's better to wait than waste.

306 BAN DRINK IN BED

Don't let your toddler take a bottle of milk or cup of juice to bed with them, even if they beg you. Going to sleep with drinks can cause dental problems, like cavities, so if they must have drinks in bed, make it plain water.

307 RESET YOUR CLOCKS

Instead of getting annoyed every time your toddler gets you up before 7am, try to reset your clock around them. The likelihood is that they're not waking up on purpose, so if they consistently wake at 6am, you'll just have to get used to it and go to bed a bit earlier yourself to compensate.

308 A NIGHT LIGHT

Some toddlers get disorientated and upset if they wake up in the middle of the night and it's pitch black. If your child is frightened of the dark, consider a night light attached to their cot/bed that they can turn on and off.

309 RECLINE THE SEAT

If you often take your child off to friends' houses and want to put them to bed in the car, make sure you get a car seat that reclines so they'll be comfortable, especially if you're going to be making long journeys.

310 BE CONSISTENT

Whatever method you decide to employ to cope with your child's night wakefulness, make sure you apply it consistently – and that means everyone does it every night. Your child will soon take advantage if the routine changes.

311 SLEEP DIARY

If your toddler's sleeping patterns are really causing you problems and they've lasted more than a month, try keeping a sleep diary for a week to make note of all the issues and approach your doctor to see whether there is a sleep clinic or specialist they can recommend.

312 STICK TO THE SCHEDULE

If your child is an early riser, resist the temptation to put them to bed later. The chances are they'll still wake up at the same time, but will have had less sleep. In fact, as counter-intuitive as it may sound, many children will wake up later if put to bed earlier.

313 DON'T DISMISS FEARS

If your child starts having nightmares, always take their fears seriously. Go to your child or take them back to bed, soothe them and explain they have had a bad dream, Give them something nice to visualize and stay with them until they are no longer afraid.

314 BLACK OUT THE WINDOWS

If come summertime, when the mornings are lighter, your child begins to wake up earlier, it might be worth investing in some black-out blinds or material to drape over the window to help them sleep longer.

315 GET AN ALARM CLOCK

If your toddler consistently wakes up very early and comes to find you or cries for attention, consider buying them a special alarm clock designed to help them know when getting up time is. Those with designs like sleeping rabbits and other animals are popular.

316 DRINK BEFORE BED

Giving your toddler a glass of warm milk before bedtime might sound like an old wives' tale, but there's some truth to it. Milk contains tryptophan, which is thought to raise serotonin levels and make you feel sleepy.

317 DOING IT ON THEIR OWN

Don't get into the habit of waiting with your child until they fall asleep. Instead, make sure they are really sleepy and comfortable and allow them to learn the last stage of actually falling asleep on their own.

318 LET THEM NAP ON

Most experts recommend napping should continue until the child is three years old. Even if they're not actually sleeping, some quiet time reading or listening to music in their bedroom can help them recharge for the afternoon.

discipline the right way

318 GIVE GOOD ATTENTION

The main reason for misbehaviour in children aged two to five is that they are attention seeking. They want your attention and they'll do anything to get it, even if it means you telling them off. As well as using discipline, try and give them more attention when they're behaving well to reinforce good behaviour.

320 USE YOUR EXPRESSIONS

When you communicate with your toddler, especially if they're doing something you want them to stop, exaggerate your facial expressions and hand movements to make your message more powerful.

321 ON THEIR LEVEL

If your child has done something wrong, don't shout at them from somewhere else in the house as your message might get lost. Instead, go to your child and get down to their level by crouching or kneeling so they can't ignore you.

322 DIG THE DISCIPLINE

Don't fall into the trap of thinking that disciplining your child will make them love you less or think that you love them less. Discipline is as much about setting positive boundaries (with praise and encouragement) as it is about discouraging negative behaviour.

323 LOOK IN THEIR EYES

If you want to tell your child something important or tell them off, hold your child by the arms so they can't run away and make sure they look at you. If they try to look away, ask them to look at you again and make sure they are making eye contact before you start talking.

324 KEEP IT LOW-KEY

Instead of shouting at your child, make your voice slow and firm. Don't plead with your child or raise your voice to them, which makes you seem less authoritative. Reserve this tone for when you are displeased and your child will soon learn to recognize it and try to avoid it.

325 WHINGEING WON'T WORK

Little goes straight through to a parent's brain quicker than whingeing, but giving in to it just to make it go away will lead to problems in the long term. Instead, calmly tell your child that you don't respond to that tone of voice and that you'll listen to them when they speak properly.

326 NO DEAL

Don't bargain with your child, especially over important behaviours like mealtimes and discipline. Children always win bargaining competitions because they don't understand the implicit 'rules'. Instead, give them clear rules and rewards.

327 STAY POSITIVE

Remember that it's not just the words you use but the emotions behind them that your child picks up on. Always using negative feelings, like 'don't put your dirty hands on the wall' does little to build confidence. Use alternatives like, 'let's wash your hands now, then you can put them wherever you like'.

328 DON'T SHOUT BACK

If your child shouts at you, don't rise to the bait – a shouting match will do little to help anyone. Instead, adopt a firm tone and tell your child not to talk to you in that manner.

329 LOOK IN THE MIRROR

If you're worried about having the authority to discipline your kids, don't be afraid to practise in front of a mirror in order to perfect your 'authoritative' tone. Or ask your partner or a friend to help you sound sterner.

330 MAKE IT A 'YES' DAY

Create a 'yes' day for your child. Every time they agree to something that you ask them to do, put a 'yes' sticker or star on a chart. At the end of the day if there are more 'yes' than 'no' stickers, they get a treat.

331 REMOVE TEMPTATION

If there are things you don't want your toddler to play with – like remote controls and DVD players – try and keep them out of immediate touching range. This might mean a high shelf or simply hiding from view.

332 HEAD THEM OFF

As your child stops being an infant and starts being a toddler, they are at their most impulsive, led by their desires. Instead of entering into lots of situations where you're telling them not to do things, try to use avoidance tactics instead and head issues off before they happen.

333 BRING ON A SUB

Instead of using negatives when you don't want your child to do something or play with a certain object, try using substitutions. For instance, 'you can't have a biscuit, but would you like some apple?' Or 'you can't play with the knife but why not bounce the ball instead?'

334 BE RIGID ON RULES

If your child is resistant to brushing their teeth before bed, teach them some basic rules such as 'no brushing, no story', and make sure you stick to it. Your child will test you on your rule at least once but if you stick to your guns, they are unlikely to keep it up.

335 USE YOUR HUMOUR

If you know you're facing a possible conflict situation – like asking your child to turn off the TV while they are watching something or coming to the dinner table when they are playing with toys – try not to treat it like a fight. Use distraction, humour, indeed anything to help your child do as you ask.

336 IGNORE THE 'NOS'

Prepare yourself to hear your child say 'no', sometimes what feels like several hundred times a day, but try not to take it personally. Their 'no' is more about them setting boundaries and exploring individuality than anything else.

337 LOWER THE TONE

Reserve a 'serious' tone of voice for when your child is doing something really dangerous or worrying. Stand still and lower the tone of your voice, speaking slowly and clearly. As long as you don't use it too often, your child will learn it means 'no nonsense'. Be calm and keep any hint of hysteria out of your voice.

338 SAY YOU ARE SORRY

All parents do things they regret sometimes. Set an example for your children by being big enough to apologize – say you're sorry, you love them and you'll try your best not to let it happen again.

toilet training

339 TIMING IS CRUCIAL

Timing is everything when it comes to toilet training. Get it right and the whole process should be a fairly easy ride, but try to force it on your child too early and you could be in for many months, if not years, of problems. Readiness is linked to language, so make sure your child can understand the principle.

340 BE A COPIED CAT

Before you start toilet training, it's essential that your child understand what it's about. Let them see you pee (if necessary, on the potty) and describe what's happening. In this way, you'll set them up to want to copy you.

341 WAIT UNTIL THEY'RE READY

Many parents are obsessed with setting timescales for toilet training. Instead of trying to fit your child to a predetermined schedule, studies show you'll have more success if you fit the schedule to the child and start when they're ready. The physical development that will allow your child bladder control happens at around 18 months, but it usually takes another year or so before they are ready.

342 THEY'LL LET YOU KNOW

One good sign that your child might be ready for potty training is if they consistently let you know (by words or actions like squatting or going to the corner of the room) that they are about to pee or poo. But make sure it's something they do regularly before you start.

343 LEARNING THE LANGUAGE

Don't even think about starting potty training if your child doesn't understand the difference between words like 'loo', 'potty', 'pants', 'dry', 'wet' and 'bathroom'. If they don't understand your commands, they'll never be able to grasp it.

344 TRAIN THEM TO UNDRESS

Start teaching your toddler to pull down their trousers (pants)/skirt and underwear and put them on again long before you start toilet training. If they learn this skill in advance, it will be one less thing for them to think about when you start toilet training for real.

345 RELEASE THE TENSION

Toilet training may be important to you, but adding tension and pressure to the process will not make it any easier for you or your child. Remember, unlike eating, sleeping and playing, there is no immediate pay-off for your child when they use the toilet, so it may take some time to get the idea.

346 OUT AND ABOUT

Some parents make themselves housebound the minute toilet training begins, but it's a better idea to expose you and your child to normal situations. Don't put a nappy (diaper) on your child for excursions; just take a travel potty and be prepared to stop wherever you are. They'll learn much quicker.

347 LOOK FOR THE SIGNS

If you're starting to toilet train your child, look for signs that they need to go – clutching their crotch or squatting are two fairly common signs that could signal it's time for a visit to the loo or potty.

348 DON'T DISTRACT

If you're using a potty to toilet train, avoid putting it in front of the television, as your child may well become distracted and forget what it's for. Try to make potty and loo visits as short and functional as possible.

349 COUNT THE FLUIDS

Make a mental note of how much fluid you give your child throughout the day and bear this in mind when it comes to toilet trips, especially in the training stages. If they are drinking a lot, chances are they'll need to pee more.

350 TOO MUCH EXCITEMENT

When it's toilet training time, most children have accidents, wet their pants and even soil themselves at some point, often at times of excitement or anxiety. Try and remain calm and not make an issue out of it, and remind them constantly to use the toilet if they need it.

351 DON'T DISCIPLINE SOILERS

Never discipline your child for soiling themselves. Usually, reverting to soiling is due to illness, fear, stress or family disruption, so your child is likely to need help and support. Explain gently how they can stop it happening in future by not trying to hold it in.

352 CAN YOU FEEL IT?

If you're trying to get your child to tell you before they need to pee, try explaining to them how it feels. Place your hand on their tummy over their bladder and say to them, 'can you feel it here?' so they know what to expect.

353 BEFORE YOU GO

Remember, if you're toilet training your child, make sure you ask them before you start a journey if they need to pee. Often, your child may be too excited about the forthcoming outing to remember, so reminding them will help prevent accidents.

354 ASK THE QUESTION

When you're trying to toilet train your child it's not enough to rely on them to come to you when they feel the urge, especially if they're involved in games or toys. Ask them if they need a pee a hundred times a day if necessary, to get the message across.

355 KEEP IT PRIVATE

Work with your child to help them use the potty. If they're naturally shy, putting the potty in the middle of the room may be off-putting for them; they may prefer a quiet corner or even the hallway.

356 FINGER ON THE TRIGGER

Bedwetting can be a sign that the night-time nappy (diaper) has been left off too soon, but it can also be a sign of anxiety or a fear of the dark. Some children will wet strange beds or if their routine is upset, so be aware of your child's triggers.

357 DON'T HOLD IT IN

Some children become anxious about bowel movements, and holding it in for too long can lead to constipation, which can cause pain and discomfort and compound the issue. Put them in a warm bath, make sure they are drinking fluids and eating enough fibre and use gentle encouragement.

358 STAY CALM

Toilet training can be fraught with emotional issues, but studies have shown that children react better and learn faster when their parents remain calm and relaxed about the process and avoid blame or anxiety if problems occur. Keep a light attitude and don't get upset about any accidents – make sure they know it's all to be expected.

359 POT THE POTTY

Many parents prefer to use the toilet straight away rather than use a potty, but some children can be frightened of the flushing toilet or of being so high up with their legs dangling. Work with your child's inclinations to decide on the best way for them.

360 A SLEEPY TOILET TRIP

If your child consistently wets the bed, try breaking the cycle by waking them up and sitting them on the toilet or potty last thing at night when you go to bed. Most children will stay half-asleep while you do this, and it might help prevent wet sheets.

361 KEEP THINGS CLEAN

Take as many opportunities as you can to bracket toilet training with hygiene. Let them try to wipe their own bottom, encourage them to wash their hands afterwards and flush the toilet.

family harmony

362 DISCUSS YOUR DECISIONS

Remember to discuss your parenting decisions and rules with your partner. If possible, make time once a week to have a brief chat about problems you've encountered and things you are worried about, then come up with solutions together and stick to them.

363 PLAN PLAN BS

Juggling the demands of work and a family can be immensely stressful, particularly if children become ill. If you can, set up 'plan Bs' in advance. Ask grandparents or friends to look after them or organize to work from home or make up time the week after if your child needs you at home.

364 GET A SITTER

Finding a sitter you trust can be difficult, especially in the evenings. If your child is at nursery or playgroup, consider asking one of the workers if they want to babysit to give you some time off. That way, your child will be looked after by someone they know and you will have peace of mind.

365 NET A NANNY

If your child is ill and you or your partner need to be away with work or can't take time off, think about employing a temporary nanny. Many nannies that work part-time are also enrolled with local agencies for 'bank' work, and are happy to look after ill children

366 FORM A BABYSITTING CLUB

Instead of spending money on babysitters every time you want to go out for a meal, why not create a babysitting club with a group of friends? That way, you can trade babysitting hours with each other for free. Or use tokens if there are enough of you that you might lose count. You can also organize it so you babysit for each other in exchange for points: each time you babysit for another member of the club you receive points, and you lose them when someone babysits for you. Making the babysitting night the same week after week allows the various families involved to plan their life ahead of time, but make sure you agree on general rules and know and trust all adults involved.

GROWING UP

building relationships

367 LISTEN, DON'T LECTURE

Be there for your child. Let them talk to your in their own way. What was their day like? What did they like best about it? Allow your child to openly express ideas, feelings and worries. Listen rather than lecturing and encourage your child to express feelings creatively by drawing or keeping a diary.

368 PLAY SIMON SAYS

Encourage your pre-schooler's social development and have fun at the same time by playing 'Simon Says'. The aim is they obey your instructions only when you prefix them with the phrase 'Simon says…'

368 MIND THEIR MANNERS

Children shouldn't feel manners are optional. Teach them from an early age that manners are a display of consideration for others, and show them how nice it is to hear them saying 'please' and 'thank you'.

370 BALANCE THE BENEFITS

If your child exhibits envy of another's house, toys, holidays (vacations) or other possessions, this is a good opportunity to teach them to see the positive side of situations. Remind them that few things are as they seem on the surface and encourage them to remember the benefits of their own situation.

371 AVOID LABELS

Labelling your pre-schooler could be a self-fulfilling prophecy. For instance, calling your daughter 'clumsy' may make her more apprehensive about picking things up and more likely to drop things; while your 'nervous' son will only become more so if he thinks it's being noticed.

372 HANG ON TO CLINGERS

If your pre-schooler is going through a clingy phrase, don't try to push them away. They will embrace independence in their own time. Encourage it by setting them small, non-challenging tasks and giving lots of praise when they achieve something.

373 DON'T TAKE THINGS PERSONALLY

Often, pre-school children will test the boundaries of their parent's love by saying things like, 'I hate you' and 'I don't love you'. This is perfectly normal. Reassure them that you love them whatever they feel about you and wait for the phase to pass.

374 TRAVEL IN TIME

If you're worried about whether you're giving your child the right messages, imagine you're 15 years in the future and your child is grown up. What would they say their main childhood messages were? If they're not positive, take measures to change them.

375 KNOW THEIR MOODS

Just like adults, children have their own unique patterns of good and bad moods during the day. Getting to know your child's pattern of behaviour is key to helping reduce conflict in the home. For instance, if they always get tired in the evenings .make sure you don't expect too much of them at that time.

376 CREATE A STICKER CHART

Older children usually respond brilliantly to star charts and stickers for good behaviour, such as 'no hitting' or 'dressing themselves'. Perhaps allow them to build up 'good behaviour' points for a small reward when they have collected, say, ten. But beware of over-rewarding your child – make sure the points match the prizes.

377 BE A TRANSLATOR

Try to translate concepts into a child's language. For instance, you could tell them that although secrets can be fun, it's never good to keep a secret that feels bad or confusing. Secrets should be good things, and if someone asks them to keep a secret that makes them feel uneasy, it's not a proper secret.

378 ANSWER HONESTLY

Pre-schoolers never seem to stop talking. By the time they're three years old, most children ask endless questions. Answer as patiently and truthfully as you can. Your responses are helping your child to learn and soon they'll realize that you don't have all the answers!

379 LINK THOUGHTS AND ACTIONS

Try to give your pre-schooler the message that you understand their feelings and aren't trying to tell them not to have feelings simply to limit behaviour. For instance, 'I understand you're angry with George for taking your ball but it's not OK to hit him.'

380 SAY 'PLAY NICELY'

Playing games with children can turn from being fun to no fun at all in seconds. Don't react with anger; simply say to your child, 'I'm going to go away until you're ready to play nicely again. Let me know when you are. I'll come back and we'll enjoy the game together.'

381 USE OPEN QUESTIONS

If you are worried that your child doesn't talk to you enough, try using open-ended questions instead of closed ones. For instance, replace 'did you have fun at school today?' with 'what was your favourite thing today?'

382 BRAIN POSITIVES

The brain doesn't work in negatives, so try to use positive commands to your children. 'Keep out of the road' will immediately bring a picture of the road into their head, making them more likely to want to go there, whereas, 'stay on the pavement (sidewalk)' is a more positive image.

383 KEEP IT SIMPLE

Start early by answering your child's questions about sex simply and keep the discussion going as they get older. Ask your child what they think, so that you know how far their knowledge goes and can give answers and advice that they can understand.

384 ASK NO QUESTIONS

By the time your pre-schooler is five or so, they will be able to answer questions like 'why did you do that?' Before that age you'll only confuse them, so it's better to use age-appropriate phrases like, 'let's think about why you did that.'

385 LIAR, LIAR

Don't worry about make-believe friends and exaggerated stories. Even downright lies are common for pre-schoolers. Don't discourage it or challenge them as it's good for their imagination, but gently introduce them to the concept of real and imaginary.

386 GIVE THEM A PRESENCE

If you are trying to get something done but your child keeps interrupting, see what happens if you offer your presence but not your attention. In other words, let your child play alongside you (for instance, with colouring or a jigsaw at the table beside you). Don't expect too much to start with and praise them if they work without interrupting you.

387 PUPPET SHOW

The best way to understand what a child feels is for them to tell you, but even outgoing children often go silent when asked. Using puppets to talk to each other can often be a less threatening way of your child expressing their feelings.

388 FACE UP TO FEELINGS

Don't shy away from addressing big emotions in your children, even if they are very young. For instance, losing a grandparent or beloved pet can be distressing. Listen to your children's feelings and try to respond appropriately.

389 MAINTAIN ATTENTION

How many times have you seen a parent talking to a child but the child's gone parent-deaf and isn't absorbing a word? Make sure the first sentence you say contains the essence of your message and avoid long explanations. If their eyes glaze over, you've lost their attention. Ask them to look at you and restate your message using short, simple words.

390 READ THEIR SIGNS

As soon as your child can express themselves emotionally, encourage them to talk to you about their feelings, and watch their body language. Learning to read your child's signs will help you understand how they're feeling without them having to explain.

391 WAITING THEIR TURN

While young toddlers find it impossible not to interrupt, pre-schoolers can begin to learn good manners. Let them know that waiting their turn is what big people do. Don't respond to interruptions – simply say 'wait until I have finished, please' and be prepared to repeat yourself.

392 LET THEM PLEASE YOU

Lots of children want to please you but don't like being ordered around. Use this to help encourage your child to be obedient. For example, say, 'Mummy would like you to go upstairs now' or 'Daddy wants you to put your hat on'.

393 CALM THEIR FEARS

If your child is frightened, acknowledge their feelings without giving them too much attention, which could encourage them to make more of a fuss. Talk in a calm voice and explain why there is nothing to be frightened of.

394 LET THEM TIME YOU

Pre-schoolers can be just as bad as toddlers at wanting attention when it's most inconvenient for you. Use their extra maturity by involving them in the waiting process. You could give them your watch and tell them that when the hand reaches a certain point, you'll put down the phone/ cooking/dishcloth and come and join them.

395 GIVE YOUR REASONS

Offer your child reasons for your request that will negate the power struggle and give them a reason to comply. For instance, say, 'Get dressed so you can go outside and play' and they will focus on the play rather than the dressing. Avoid giving them lengthy and abstract reasons; no matter how reasonable they will find these difficult to grasp.

396 SPECIAL TREATMENT

Create special kisses or cuddles for your child, so they have something from you nobody else gets. For instance, kiss them on the ears, nose, mouth and forehead in that order, and reserve that particular routine especially for them.

397 BE GRATEFUL

As adults, we often forget to be grateful for the things we have in life rather than worrying about the things we don't. Set your child up for positive thinking in later life by telling them what you are grateful for and ask them about their feelings too.

398 REPEAT YOUR REQUESTS

If your child consistently doesn't comply with your requests, ask them to repeat it back to you. If they can't, it could be that it was too long and complicated. Try making it simpler and repeating it often.

TV time

399 FIGHT THE FEAR

Don't let your children watch TV programmes that frighten them. Children under five often mix up fantasy and reality, so programmes like the news can scare them. Keep an eye on what they're watching and adjust their viewing accordingly.

400 AVOID OVERSTIMULATION

Limit your child's television watching in the run-up to bedtime. It's often difficult for children to unwind in front of the TV so choosing books and quiet games is better. Don't let them have a TV or computer game in their bedroom.

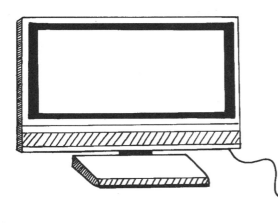

402 TOT UP THEIR SCREEN TIME

Don't just count television watching as screen time. Working on the computer and playing computer games also count. Ideally, you should try to reduce the time your children spend staring at a screen and encourage them to be active.

401 TAKE CONTROL OF THE TV

In some homes the TV is on all day long and the children are left to supervise their own viewing. This has been shown to reduce school performance, concentration and behaviour. Take control of the remote so that you are in charge of their viewing matter and time.

403 SOLVE SOME PROBLEMS

Television, films and radio entertain children, but they don't engage the part of the brain that solves problems or thinks creatively or critically. Boost development by creating games based around their favourite programmes to encourage thought.

404 TEACH THEM TO CONCENTRATE

Make a simple rule that the TV doesn't go on without there being a programme they want to watch. As they get a little older, extend the rule – if they can't tell you the name of the character or the programme or what it's about, it goes off.

405 DON'T GET GOGGLE-EYED

New guidelines suggest no TV viewing at all before the age of two or three, but TV viewing is a fact of life for most modern families. As long as the TV isn't your babysitter, don't beat yourself up about it.

being prepared

406 DO A DRILL

Just as your children undergo regular emergency drills at pre-school and school, make sure they know what to do at home if there is a fire or other emergency. Walk them through the steps they should take and have regular drills.

407 GET A KIT TOGETHER

Prepare an emergency kit that your family can use. Let the children help you collect items and pack them in a box or bag. Include a torch or flashlight, battery-operated radio, a few cans of food and so on.

408 PREPARE FOR DISASTER

Around the time they start school, your child may begin to have worries about things like fire, flood and storms. Help them feel secure by talking to them about their fears and helping them feel prepared with emergency kits and drills.

shopping

409 PLAN AHEAD

If you have to take your child shopping, plan ahead. Pick a time of day when your child is most amenable and you're feeling on top of things. Write a list and, if possible, match the list to the route you'll take around the store so it won't take you too long.

410 GET A SHOPPING ASSISTANT

Let your child help you in the supermarket. Give them their own little list and let them go round the aisles with you and fill up their own space in the trolley (shopping cart) or basket. If they are involved, they are less likely to act up.

411 STRAP THEM IN

If your child is restless in the trolley (shopping cart) as you shop in the supermarket, consider either taking them out (and using a harness or leash to keep them nearby) or making sure they wear the safety straps. Falling out could cause them serious injury.

412 LET THEM EAT FRUIT!

Most supermarkets have their fruit and vegetable department at the front of the store. Use this to your advantage by giving your child a healthy snack to chew on as you start your shopping, avoiding demands for crisps (potato chips), sweets (candy) and chocolate later on.

413 DON'T SHOP IN SILENCE

Don't forget that conversations you have with your child while shopping can be really helpful in educating them about food and other items, as well as boosting their language and social skills.

414 SHOP TILL YOU DROP

Too small to be left alone and too big for the trolley (shopping cart) seat, shopping trips with pre-schoolers can be a real nightmare. Try some gradual training – start them off in the trolley, then holding hands, then resting your hand on their shoulder. Praise them every 30 seconds to 1 minute for being so good, and gradually they will learn.

415 KEEP TRIPS SHORT

Why not leave the children at home when you have a long shopping list? Or get the basics online and save shopping with your kids for those few items when you can run in and out and keep the trip short. Often, long trips exhaust everyone's patience.

dealing with discipline

416 SAY 'WHEN' NOT 'IF'

Use the word 'when' rather than the word 'if' when you're instructing your child. For instance, 'when you've finished brushing your teeth, then we can read the book'. Saying 'if' implies they have a choice.

417 BE SPECIFIC

Try to avoid giving your children vague directions, like 'be good' or 'behave yourself', which are open to interpretation. It's far easier for them to do as you ask if you give them specifics, like 'we do not throw food around and we sit at the table to eat our meal'. And make sure you praise them when they do.

418 MAKE A RHYME

To get your child to remember your house rules, make them into rhymes. For instance, 'if I hit, then I sit' will remind them they will have a 'time out' if they hit anyone.

419 DON'T WIMP OUT

Although discipline usually comes more easily to one parent than the other, resist the urge to play 'good cop, bad cop'. Threats like 'wait till your father gets home' won't mean anything to a pre-schooler, who needs to be punished there and then for the relevance to sink in.

420 AVOID DOUBLE DISCIPLINE

When one parent is disciplining a child, they will often run to the other parent. If your child runs to you, the best thing to do is to take them back to the other parent rather than getting involved yourself. This reinforces your joint parenting.

421 FOLLOW IT THROUGH

If you say 'no' to your child, make sure you both understand what that means and keep to the rule. Then act quickly (within seconds rather than minutes) when it is challenged. Always carry out any threatened punishment so your child knows that 'no' means 'no' (this also means thinking before you threaten something – do you really want to leave the restaurant if they don't start behaving?!).

422 CHOOSE THE MOST VALUED

Confiscating favourite toys can be a good way to back up discipline for your pre-schooler but it won't work if they can easily replace it with another toy. Make sure you choose toys that mean something to them or the process won't hold value.

423 LET THEM GET BETTER

Don't tell your child off if they're ill or recovering from illness. Sick children often behave badly without being able to help themselves, so if they're coming down with something be more lenient.

424 DON'T BE DIVIDED

Try not to fall into the trap of using discipline when it's unclear exactly what happened between two children. Most children will tell the truth about what happened but if a child is repeatedly told off for something that wasn't their fault they may begin to lie.

425 LET THEM LEARN LESSONS

Go easy on disciplining your child if their behaviour has given them a shock or hurt them. For example, if they've been warned not to touch something that's fallen on the floor it might be upsetting. Chances are they've already learned the hard way, so talking to them about what happened and reminding them of the rules may be enough.

426 BREAK UP THE FIGHT

If children are playing together in a room and the play is spiralling out of control, break it up before it breaks down completely. You might need to separate them or simply call them into the kitchen for a drink of water. Anything to give them a chance to calm down.

427 CHANGE THE ROUTINE

If there are particular activities – like hair washing or tooth brushing – that always cause problems for your child, try removing them from their normal place in the routine and doing them at another time of day. It will probably still be difficult but sometimes it's easier to break the pattern.

428 DON'T HOLD A GRUDGE

Even if you're still angry with your child, make yourself praise them if they apologize for something they've done wrong so they know the incident is over. Make sure your child doesn't pick up any 'irritated' vibes once their punishment is over.

429 GET A FULL APOLOGY

Don't just accept a single word apology if your child has done something wrong. Make sure they understand what they're saying sorry for by asking them to give you a full apology. For instance, 'I'm sorry for punching Jane'.

430 TEACH RESPECT

It's important that older children learn some respect for their belongings and for those of other people. Help them do this by not always buying them a new toy every time you go to the store and helping them to understand that everything has its own value.

431 GIVE THEM COMMANDS

Instead of using the word 'no', which doesn't really mean anything to a young child, try using words that they associate with meaning and can act on. 'Stop', 'freeze', 'wait', 'leave it', 'drop it' and so on, are all words a young child can respond to, and if they do you can praise them.

432 THINK BEFORE YOU SPEAK

Beware what you threaten your children with in anger. You want them to know you are consistent so it's important to carry out threats whenever you issue them. Think before you speak and try to issue threats that you are happy to carry out.

433 STRIKE A BALANCE

Try to strike a balance between the amount of times you say 'yes' and 'no' during the day. If you're not sure if you've got the balance, use a jotter pad to count up your 'yeses' and 'nos' over the course of a day and see if you're hitting a balance.

434 NOT THE BEDROOM

Some people send children to their bedrooms when they have been naughty but many experts believe this is a mistake because bedrooms should be seen as places of comfort and sanctuary rather than punishment. Also, there is usually quite a lot to entertain a child in a bedroom. A hallway, kitchen or a corner of a room are better places for a time out.

435 THROW THEM A LOOK

Develop a 'look' that will let your child know you want them to stop their behaviour without you having to say 'no' all the time. Try standing still, raising your eyebrows and pursing your lips to communicate displeasure.

436 ACT AND SPEAK

Body language can be a great way to reinforce what you're saying to get your child to stop certain kinds of behaviour. Putting your hands on your hips and holding up a hand as if to say 'stop' are both good ways of stopping them in their tracks. Avoid mixed messages – telling your child they are misbehaving while hugging and smiling for example.

437 APPROPRIATE 'NO'

Aim to help your child use the word 'no' appropriately. You don't want them to say 'no' to everything you suggest but at the same time, you want them to be confident enough to say 'no' if there is something they really don't want to do.

428 GET RID OF THE TOY

If your children fight over toys or belongings, a powerful way to enforce your message of sharing is to remove the toy or object altogether and make sure they both know why it's being removed.

439 SING A STOP SOUND

Instead of using words like 'no' all the time, try to develop a repertoire of 'stop that' sounds. Those that work best are hard, repeated sounds in the back of your throat like 'ah-ah' and 'uh-uh'.

dressing up

440 MAKE PRACTICAL CHOICES

When you're out shopping for clothes for your child, make sure you think about practicalities as well as how they look. Avoid fiddly poppers and buttons and choose clothes that are comfortable around the neck and arms.

441 CHOOSE COMFORTABLE CLOTHES

There is a difference between your child refusing to wear certain clothes one day and consistently refusing to put on a certain item on the grounds of discomfort, i.e. if a top is too tight or trousers (pants) rub. Don't make your children wear clothes they aren't comfortable in.

442 ALLOW INDIVIDUALITY

Pre-schoolers do not have open minds to alternatives! If they've decided they want to wear the striped blue trousers with the spotty orange top, let them, even if it's not to your taste. It's good to allow them some individuality.

443 PLAY A TRICK

Trick your child into having fun rather than resisting. For instance, if your child won't get dressed, surprise them by taking all your clothes off and have a race with them to see who can get dressed first. They'll soon forget their resistance.

444 PRAISE SELF-DRESSING

Encourage your child to learn to dress themselves, then there will be less arguments about what they are wearing. If they are being praised for doing well at self-dressing, there will be less incentive for them to act up for attention.

445 LIMIT CHOICE

Try not to get caught up in arguments about clothes with your young child. Offering them too many choices may simply confuse them, so try to limit the options you give them. Allow them some choice, but don't get caught up in bickering.

446 YOUNG SHOPAHOLIC

Aged around four or five, children start to want to exert control over what they wear. Let them make some of the decisions when you shop by choosing one of three dresses or pairs of trousers (pants). Or give them a choice of two pairs of shoes.

447 CHANGE THE RECORD

A great tip for getting your child dressed with no fuss is to play games or sing songs to engage them and distract them from what you are trying to do. Encourage them to sing and make small movements in time to the music.

448 DOING IT THEMSELVES

Help your child dress themselves as early as you can, even if it means the process takes longer. Young children can lift up a leg, older children can put on their shirt while you button it and school-aged children can button shirts and coats and tie shoes.

time out

449 TIME IT OUT

Once your child is old enough, you can begin to introduce a 'time out' area. This could be a chair, a step in the hall or a kitchen corner, but should be somewhere where there are no toys to distract them or to allow them to enjoy it. For this reason, avoid using bedrooms, playrooms or gardens. There are special time-out chairs available, and these are beneficial as they are hardback and easy for the child to distinguish from ordinary furniture.

450 WARM UP TO WARNING

Make sure you don't use time out without warning your child. Give them clear directions, 'if you don't … you'll have to take time out' and give them a chance to comply. You may like to use a 'count of five' principle, holding up five fingers and giving a countdown because this will visually clue them in. If they don't comply, take them quickly and firmly to the time-out seat, and tell them how long you're going to keep them there for and set a timer. If they are still shouting or screaming at the end, return to them and explain that time out won't end until they are quiet.

451 KEEP THEM STILL

If your child continually hops up and down during time out and won't stay put, sit down with them and gently but firmly keep them there. Don't talk, shout or otherwise engage with them in any way and let them know they will not leave the time out until they stay there on their own.

452 GIVE THEM A SECOND CHANCE

If not following an instruction was the reason for giving your child time out, offer them a chance to do so after time out has finished, and praise or reward them when they do. Juxtaposing punishment and reward like this reinforces the message.

453 TAKE TIME OUT SERIOUSLY

Don't treat time out as a prison sentence or act as if it's a hard punishment for your child, which might make them even more upset. Instead, treat it as some time for them to think about their actions and calm down.

454 LEAVE THEM ALONE

Don't let other siblings or children interrupt your child's time out. It's important they spend the time alone reflecting on what they've done. Tell other children about what has happened and how long they have to leave the child alone for, then take them to another room or area.

455 TAKE A TIME OUT

Bear in mind that you may need a time out as much as your child, especially if things have become heated and difficult. If you feel your temper rising, don't be afraid to give yourself a time out, and let your child see you do it.

456 PRAISE WHEN NECESSARY

Don't forget that the concept of 'time out' actually stems from psychologists, who used it as a 'time out from positive reinforcement', meaning the withdrawal of positive parental attention. For it to work properly, you need to give your kids lots of attention when they are behaving well so they recognize the absence of attention.

457 GRADE THE TIME OUTS

Help children grade bad behaviour by setting time outs for older kids based on the severity of what they've done. For instance, you might give your kids a 1-minute time out if they're getting too boisterous but up it to 5 if one of them has punched or kicked the other – they will learn to recognize the severity of their misbehaviour.

458 THINK WHILE YOU WAIT

If your child is taking time out, don't just forget about it. Spend the time they are there thinking about their behaviour and how you dealt with it, and planning what to say to them to help them go through the reflection and apology.

459 TIME OUT OUTSIDE

Time out doesn't only have to be for bad behaviour at home. Park benches, the back seat of the car and a boring corner of the store can all be suitable time-out places to help your child calm down and reflect on their behaviour.

460 TIME TO TIME

If you're trying to make your child take time out and they won't sit on the chair or step, tell them calmly and firmly that time out will not start until they sit down. Use a kitchen timer or stop watch: if they move around, stop the timer, wait until they settle and then re-start it. Try to ignore crying, shouting and insults; it is simply due to frustration.

461 START EARLY

Some parents start second and third children on time out as early as 18 months. Younger siblings will often grasp concepts more quickly than their older brothers and sisters because they have seen it in action so many times before.

medical matters

462 GET SOME HELP

If your child has an allergic reaction to food it is most likely to show up as red itching skin, diarrhoea and vomiting. In this case, avoiding the food is usually enough. If your child ever gets signs of serious allergy, like swollen lips or shortness of breath, you should seek medical help straight away.

463 ARM YOURSELF WITH ARNICA

Arnica is a great natural remedy for bruises and bumps. Use it as a gel, cream or lotion, applied once or twice a day to help little arms and legs heal more quickly if they're bruised or marked.

464 RAISE THE TEMPERATURE

If you tell your doctor the temperature of your child, make sure you also tell them where you took it (that is, the armpit, ear, forehead, tongue or rectum) as parts of the body can make at least a degree of difference. The normal temperature for a child as measured in the mouth varies from 36.5 to 37.2°C (97.7–99°F) and a fever means having a body temperature of at least .5°C (32.9°F) above normal on two recordings, taken at least two hours apart.

465 LOOSEN THEIR CLOTHES

One thing you can do to help your children if they come down with chicken pox is to make sure they wear loose, comfortable clothing and try to give them time out of clothing for the spots to dry (and out of nappies (diapers) if appropriate).

466 COMB IT OUT

Most children will get headlice at some point in their life. Use a fine louse comb with some natural herbal powders or lotion to remove them and check at least once a day for a week.

467 PUT THEM OFF WITH PONG

Once you've got rid of lice, keep your child's head louse free by adding a couple of drops of tea tree oil to a bottle of shampoo – the critters hate the smell!

468 DON'T LET THE BEDBUGS BITE

Vacuuming your child's mattress to get rid of dead skin and dust mite debris whenever you change their sheets can help reduce night-time contaminants, helping to reduce allergies, wheezing and runny noses at night by purifying the air.

469 CALM THE ITCH

For skin rashes and itching due to chicken pox, try calamine and aqueous cream or Eurax cream – they are easier to apply than watery lotions and work straight away to cool down skin and prevent itching.

home sweet home

470 ACCEPT THE DAMAGE

Children are notoriously difficult to control, and it will be tiresome spending your whole life at home telling them they can't touch things. Try to invest in surfaces and objects that don't need constant upkeep (or leaving alone) to look good; that way you can keep the 'don't touches' to a minimum.

471 SLIP IN A MAT

Put a rubber mat down in your bath so your child doesn't slip, especially if you use the shower. This is particularly important if you get them to stand to rinse them off at the end. Slipping in the bath can be really dangerous.

472 GIVE THEM A JOB

Get your child involved in what you're doing. Even older children don't find chores boring like adults do, so letting them help you (by choosing appropriate tasks like holding the dustpan and brush or stirring cake mixture) will help them feel involved.

473 CAR WASH SESSION

Let your pre-schoolers create their very own car wash in your kitchen. Put down protective matting (like an old shower curtain) and a bucket of water. Let them wash their toy vehicles with sponges, bubbles and spray bottles. This is a fun way of teaching them to take care of their possessions.

474 HOUSE OF HAZARDS

Your home might feel safe and secure to you, but many more accidents happen at home where parents sometimes don't realize the threats or are maybe more relaxed about supervision than when they are out. Get a friend to take a look around your home and suggest possible hazards.

475 WASH AND WEAR

One of the best investments you can make when you've got children running around your house are washable fabrics and covers – sofas, chairs, tables, curtains, rugs – it will be much easier to keep your house looking good if you can put things in the washing machine rather than investing in professional cleaning.

rules & routines

476 BE CONSISTENT

A clear routine and rules that are consistently adhered to help a child feel safe and secure, so establishing a reliable routine for your family is important. Clear-cut rules help a child learn what is right and wrong.

477 KEEP RULES TO A MINIMUM

When it comes to living as peacefully as possible with your child or children, fewer rules are better than many. Particularly when they are younger, forget about minor behaviour and concentrate on major rules like no hitting, and then bring in more rules as your child develops.

478 GIVE A WARNING

Even if children understand their routine, if they get carried away with playing or running around, they'll soon forget what is due to happen next: Give them regular warnings, 'bathtime in 5 minutes', 'bathtime in 2 minutes' and so on, to help them adjust and cut down on tantrums.

479 THE RIGHT RULES

One of the most common parental mistakes is to expect higher levels of understanding than their children are capable of. If you set appropriate rules for their abilities they are more likely to stick to them.

480 ADJUST YOUR SCHEDULE

Most children have jobs they do fast and jobs they do slowly, and routines should reflect this. For instance, if your child takes ages to wake up or is a slow dresser, make time for that in their schedule so that you're not always fighting against it.

481 PLAN YOUR EVENINGS

Most experts agree that having an evening routine is key to helping your child get themselves off to sleep happily and avoid evening stress. Most suggest supper, bath, pyjamas reading (and milk if appropriate), teeth brushing and bed.

482 GET A BOOST

Invest in a booster stool or a set of steps so they can wash their own hands and rinse their own toothbrush at the basin (bathroom sink). Children respond much better to activities if they feel they are doing it 'properly' rather than being told what to do.

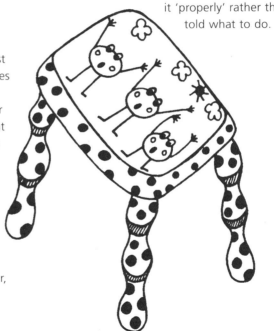

483 DO THEIR ROUTINE

If your child resists everyday activities such as hair brushing, tooth brushing and washing hands, let them see you do it regularly. Once they realize that it is part of your daily ritual and not something you're simply making them do, they should be less resistant to doing it themselves.

484 MAKE BATHTIME FUN TIME

Some children really don't like getting into the bath. Don't force them; instead try to find out what they are worried about. Make bathtime fun with songs and games and never force your child to do something they are frightened of. Try showers and body baths instead.

485 DON'T BE PLAYED

Behaviours that many parents call 'playing up', like screaming, pouting, crying for attention, showing off and arguing, are often hard not to be drawn in by. Often, they are designed to get your attention, so not giving that attention can work very well at reducing them.

486 GO ALONG WITH RITUALS

Pay attention and respect to your child's rituals. If they always want to say 'goodbye' in the same way when you leave them at nursery or school for instance, it probably means they're using the ritual as a way to minimize separation anxiety. Work with them.

487 TURN YOUR BACK

Ignoring can be a useful way of indicating that you do not want your child to do certain things. It can be a way to avoid getting into an argument and clearly shows you are not pleased. Ignoring involves no physical, verbal or eye contact until good behaviour starts.

488 JOIN A CONSULTANCY

Make sure you consult with your children's other caregivers on rules and regulations. If everyone makes up their own rules it can be very confusing for the child, so make sure at least the major rules are consistent.

489 LET OTHERS SPOIL

While it's important for caregivers to attempt to stick to the same rules and be consistent with your child's routine, it doesn't have to be completely rigid. Allowing grandparents to be a bit softer and make some of their own decisions will help make their relationship with your child special, so don't be too worried if they 'spoil' them a bit more than you do.

490 RESPECT, MAN

Teach your children to respect the rights, bodies and properties of other people. It's worth reminding them if you ask them not to do something that a lot of the 'rules' you set are about respecting other people. Reminding them of the consequences of their actions will reinforce the rule.

491 DON'T ACCEPT VIOLENCE

There are certain behaviours that should never be countenanced, including those that harm other people, such as kicking, biting and punching. Make sure your children know this is wrong and that it's unacceptable to hurt anyone else.

492 STICK TO BOUNDARIES

When it comes to setting boundaries, bear in mind that you're trying to find the middle balance between being too strict (and breaking your child's spirit) and setting enough limits that they learn to control themselves. Children who get away with everything often have problems later in life.

493 DON'T GIVE IN TO GUILT

Never forget that you aren't doing your child any favours if you indulge them in an attempt to overcome your guilty feelings (if you've spent a long time at work or been away on a trip, etc). What children need most is consistency, so don't be tempted to relax the rules.

494 WORK WITH YOUR PARTNER

There's nothing better for your child's self-esteem and security than to feel their family is a safe, stable unit. Seeing their parents helping each other around the house helps reinforce this feeling of stability, so working with your partner is a great idea. It will also give them a sense of how teamwork operates.

495 USE THEIR NAME

If you're trying to get your child's attention, use their name first in the sentence. Then, when they're looking at you and listening, say what you want to say. For instance, 'Josh, come for your bath please' will work better than 'Come for your bath please, Josh'.

496 MANNERS MATTER

Age three to five is the prime time for teaching your child good manners. Generally, they like and understand rules and love to master new skills and be praised for it. Emphasize 'magic' words and help them learn table manners. Try for a few rules at a time, though, so you don't overwhelm them.

497 VARY YOUR TREATS

Don't fall into the trap of only giving food as a reward. It's fine once in a while, but remember to reward your child with time and activities as well. For instance, instead of a cookie take them to the park for half an hour of one-on-one time.

498 HELP THEM APOLOGIZE

Encourage your child to apologize for something when they are feeling sorry. Try to get them to say why they are sorry, or let them write a note if they are uncomfortable apologizing face to face. They need to identify the reason for the apology, rather than just use the word 'sorry'.

boosting ability

498 THINK OF TIMING

As your children get older and settle in at nursery school or school, they start to understand time a bit better. Encourage this by playing 'ongoing' games with them. For instance, write a story one sentence a day or build something bit by bit.

500 GIVE THEM A CUDDLE

Use every opportunity to play games like chase and tickle with your child. Studies have shown that children who have lots of physical contact with parents are better adjusted adults, so take the opportunity to have fun!

501 LAND OF MAKE-BELIEVE

Three-year-olds are just discovering the joys of imagination. Use their love of make-believe to help get them to go along with some of your chores. For example, pretend to be different characters when you're getting them dressed or tidying up and they'll have more fun.

502 READ IT RIGHT

Parents often read to their children while their child sits on their knee, but some children don't like this, as they prefer to see your face. If your child keeps turning around, try another position like lying on the floor or sitting side by side.

503 BOOKS YOU LIKE

Make sure you enjoy your children's books. They'll soon pick it up in the tone of your voice and your behaviour if you're bored by them, and they'll get bored too, so choose stories you find appealing and vary the books to keep them fresh.

504 BOOK A CONVERSATION

Don't just read to your child but talk to them about what's going on in the story and give them time to respond. Remember, their response times will be much slower than yours so it might take a lot longer. Be patient and wait for their comments and ideas. You could even try looking at picture books, with no words, to encourage language development.

505 BOOK SOME QUIET TIME

Reading with your child can be a magical time; often it's the only time in the day when they actually sit still. Choose a quiet place where there are no distractions from TV, radio or other children, and enjoy sharing some quiet time.

506 LEAD TO READ

The best way to encourage your child to read is to lead by example. Show them that you enjoy books, magazines and newspapers. It's good for them to see that reading is valued and enjoyed regularly in the home.

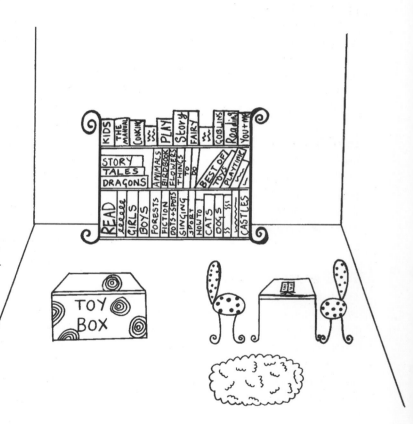

507 WORDS ARE EVERYWHERE

Don't forget that reading isn't just about stories in books – TV guides, cookery books, food labels, washing labels and wildlife books are all great ways to encourage reading and help your child get used to doing it every day.

sleeping tight

508 TIME FOR SLEEP

Even at age five, it's estimated that a quarter of children still have a daytime nap a couple of times a week, so don't worry if your child is often tired in the middle of the day. Make time in their schedules for sleep as well as activity.

509 NOT MISSING ANYTHING

If your child is resistant to naps in the daytime, it may be because they are reluctant to miss out on something that might happen while they are asleep. Tell them you'll be reading your book/sleeping/resting at the same time and they are less likely to complain.

510 THINK OF THE FUTURE

From time to time, your child will not feel sleepy at bedtime and may want to stay up. If you give in, they are likely to want a repeat performance every time they don't feel sleepy, so bear this in mind before you start bad habits like letting them come downstairs or into your bedroom.

511 GIVE THEM KISSES

Many children – especially when they get to pre-school age – will spurn kisses and cuddles from their parents during the day. Make up for it by lavishing attention on them at bedtime when they are less likely to refuse, and send them off to sleep feeling warm and secure.

512 BREATHE IT OUT

If your child has trouble getting back to sleep if they wake up at night, teach them some 'sleep' exercises, like breathing into different part of their body, or visualizations, to help their bodies and minds relax. If you do this regularly enough, they should be able to do them on their own.

513 UP THE WOODEN HILL

Aim to have at least the last part of the bedtime routine in the room in which your child sleeps. That way, they begin to associate being in their room with starting to feel sleepy, and are more likely to sleep well.

514 SET SLEEP EXPECTATIONS

Don't expect your child to sleep as much as when they were younger. Set realistic bed and nap times, allowing roughly 12 hours at three years and 11 hours at five years.

515 CHECK FOR INFECTIONS

If your older child suddenly starts bedwetting after a dry period, the most likely cause is that a stress or emotional problem has caused anxiety. Another fairly common cause is a urinary infection, so seek medical advice.

516 MASSAGE AWAY STRESS

If your child has trouble winding down, think about introducing some massage before bedtime. All children love being touched, and using oils infused with lavender or camomile can help create a calmer environment.

517 TOO TIRED

Night terrors are horrible for the child and can be almost as terrifying for the parents, but experts suggest that night terrors and nightmares are more likely if children are overtired. Putting them to bed earlier may help.

518 NO TEASE PLEASE

Never allow teasing about bedwetting, whatever age your child, and if they are older make sure you are discreet about who you tell so they aren't embarrassed by other people finding out about it. Be supportive at all times.

519 CULL THE CAFFEINE

Don't let your children drink caffeinated or high sugar drinks in the evening that might give them a 'buzz' and prevent healthy sleep. Instead, choose water, milk or diluted juice.

520 DON'T REWARD WETTING

When older children wet their beds, it can be upsetting for them as well as their parents. Make sure you react calmly and don't reward the behaviour by, for instance, allowing them to get into bed with you.

safe & secure

521 KEEP YOUR CHILDREN WITH YOU

Children in this age group shouldn't be allowed out on their own, as they are not able to take responsibility for themselves, so don't leave them unattended in public places. At this age they can be sidetracked by a task and get lost or go off with someone else.

522 STICK TOGETHER

Never leave children unsupervised in play areas, stores or parks – make sure you can always see them. Also, never leave them in cars outside stores, even if they're asleep or you're only going to be a few minutes. Always take them into the store with you.

523 A CLEAR MESSAGE

Make sure you give your children the clear message that they never have to do anything they don't like or go anywhere alone with an older adult or child, even if it's someone they know. Reinforce this at home by not making them hug or kiss people they don't want to.

524 ARRANGE A MEETING PLACE

In busy public places, arrange somewhere safe to meet in case you get separated, like an information desk or cash point, so your child will know what to do if they get lost. Remind them as you enter the store of your 'lost' plan and take them to the allocated waiting place. Don't assume they will remember from trip to trip.

525 LEND A LISTENING EAR

Listen to your children, especially when they are trying to tell you about things that worry them, for instance if there is a bully at school or a babysitter they don't like. Let them know you will always take them seriously and do whatever you can to keep them safe.

526 JUST SAY 'NO'

Give your children permission to say 'no' to anyone who asks them to do something they know or feel is wrong. Teach them to say 'no' firmly and loudly, then to go and tell another adult. Tell them they never have to keep quiet if something feels wrong and should always tell an adult.

527 CITY LIMITS

Try to set your children reasonable limits and expand them as they get older. For instance, in the park with your pre-schooler use trees or flower-beds as boundaries they can't go past; let them do what they want within them.

528 PRACTISE SAFETY RULES

Start teaching children simple rules about personal safety. Tell them clearly that they must never go off with anyone, not even someone they know, without first asking you or the adult who is looking after them. Let them practise this when you pick them up from nursery.

529 CHOOSE A UNIFORM

Very early on, children can distinguish uniforms from other types of clothing. Teach them that if they get lost, they should approach someone in uniform and tell them their name and what has happened. If they can't find someone in uniform, tell them to next approach someone with a young child.

530 MAKE A FEW VISITS

If your child is expressing concern about starting nursery or pre-school, visit it with them at different times of day to show them what happens. Remind them how many things they enjoy doing will be available there and talk to them about other children they know who enjoy their pre-school.

531 HOME IS WHERE THE HEART IS

As soon as children are old enough, teach them their full name, address and telephone number or buy them a bracelet or locket containing this information that they can wear in public. Practise these with them until they know them off by heart.

532 ALWAYS SAY GOODBYE

Never sneak away from your child or leave the room without saying goodbye. If you let them watch you go and say goodbye, they will feel more confident that you will come back than if you simply disappear, which could frighten them.

533 SACRED SPACE

It's never too early to begin respecting your child's privacy. Let them have their own space where nobody else is allowed without their permission. This can be their own bedroom but if your children must share, it can be their own bed or cupboard. Children also benefit from somewhere like a treehouse or secret outdoor space in the garden that is a 'no adults allowed' space, where they can retreat either alone or with their friends.

534 BUILD THEM UP

Research has shown that children who are more confident are less likely to be approached by bullies and dangerous adults. Build up your child's self-esteem and confidence with lots of love, praise and affection.

dealing with anger

535 CHOOSE TO IGNORE

Ignoring can be a powerful tool in stopping unwanted behaviours. Often, children will quickly lose interest in their 'naughty' act if it doesn't elicit a response from you. Instead, try making them sit quietly on their own for a few minutes, without play or conversation, to think about their actions.

536 TAKE A TIME OUT

Don't be afraid to take a time out yourself if you feel you need it. Children often make parents extremely angry but try to resist the temptation to blow your top. Instead, take a few deep breaths and think about why you are so angry. Try to identify the real problem.

537 SIGN A PACT

Make a 'stress pact' with one of your close friends – preferably one who has similar aged children – getting in contact regularly to check your stress levels. Agree to have each other's children if either of you need a break (or meet up together if you both do!).

538 SAY YOU'RE SORRY

Don't be afraid to apologize to your child. Saying something like, 'I'm sorry, what you did was naughty but I shouldn't have shouted at you. I'm feeling a bit tired, but it was wrong of me', will teach them how to apologize when they do something wrong themselves.

539 DIRECT YOUR ANGER

It's not just smacking children that's unhelpful. Try to avoid shouting at your children in anger as well as hitting. Be very careful not to criticize or put them down. If they break a rule, tell them what they did wrong and why that makes you angry. Let them know you are angry at what they did, NOT who they are.

540 KEEP YOUR HANDS TO YOURSELF

Research has shown that hitting your child does not help, and can do more damage than good because it reinforces bad behaviour rather than teaching good behaviour. Try especially to avoid striking your child in anger as it sends negative signals about how to deal with emotion.

541 ASK FOR HELP

It's common for parents to feel angry, upset or overwhelmed, particularly if they're trying to deal with more than one child. If you recognize yourself beginning to feel frustrated, ask for help. Call someone to let off steam, leave your children with someone trustworthy and go for a walk, or simply go out and meet a friend.

eating well

542 DON'T COMPARE APPETITES

How much your child eats may be very different from how much another child eats. Don't worry if it seems that your child doesn't eat enough at one meal. Children often make up for a small meal or a missed meal at the next mealtime.

543 JUDGE THEIR GROWTH

You'll know your child is eating enough if they are growing at the right rate. Talk to your doctor if you have any concerns about how your child is growing. If their growth rate is normal then don't worry if they don't seem to eat as much as you think they should.

544 KEEP COOL WITH FRUIT

If you are visiting a climate that is a lot warmer than they are used to, expect your child to eat less and drink more. Try offering fruit such as melon and other watery food as snacks and don't make an issue if they don't eat as much.

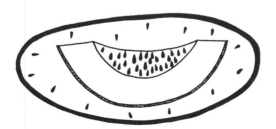

125

545 TICKLE THEIR TASTE BUDS

Try to let your child explore new foods and tastes on their own rather than trying to force them. Sometimes they may want to eat a particular food all the time and then not touch it for a while. As long as they're eating nutritiously, try not to worry.

546 SMOTHER IT IN SAUCE

According to research, children don't have as much saliva as adults. To help them and make the most of your child's love for dipping, offer them sauces and accompaniments with their meal. Salad dressings, apple sauce, cheese sauce, tomato sauce, yogurt and custard are all good favourites.

547 IN THE MEALTIME MOOD

Kids love feeling they are involved in meal-making, so choose family meals that everyone can feel hands-on with. Taco shells, fajita wraps, pitta pockets and homemade pizzas are all great choices.

548 NO COMMENT

Why not make it a family rule that nobody is allowed to say 'yuck' or make negative remarks about food on the table? If they don't like it, they should tell you calmly or simply leave it on their plate.

549 A SMOOTH TOUCH

Help your children make their own fruit and vegetable smoothies. It's a great way to get them to eat more healthy foods, and coming up with their own combinations encourages them to think about flavour.

550 FREEZE SOME FRUIT

For a cooling summer snack when your kids have been running around getting hot, why not freeze slices of fruit? Mango, peach and pineapple are all good choices but avoid watermelon as it turns very icy.

551 SPRINKLE THEIR PUD

Keep some cake decorating sprinkles in your cupboard to tempt your child to eat up their pudding. It's amazing how much better a bowl of fruit and natural yogurt looks with a shake or two of sprinkles on top.

552 SEND A WARNING SIGN

Warn your child about mealtimes 5 or 10 minutes in advance and try to get them involved. If they can help prepare food or lay the table they will feel much more engaged with the meal process.

553 AGE MATTERS

Make sure you don't expect manners that are too advanced for your child's age. A three-year-old probably won't use the right cutlery, for instance.

554 SWEETEN THEM UP

Although children shouldn't have unrestricted access to sweets (candy), a small treat as part of an otherwise healthy and well-balanced diet is fine. Experts warn that if you don't allow your kids to have any sweets, they may become 'forbidden fruits' – and then they'll do anything to get their hands on them.

555 LEAVING THE TABLE

For children aged over three it's worth teaching them some basic table manners, like no getting down from the table until they're finished (except for toilet visits). Encourage them to say, 'please may I get down?' when they have finished eating.

556 KEEP TOYS FOR TODDLERS

As your children get older, you can start to expect them to be able to concentrate on eating without employing toys, crayons and other diversions, but many toddlers need distraction at the table to keep them interested. Don't take toys away too soon or the distraction will be down to you.

557 A TRANQUIL TABLE

If mealtimes are pleasant, your child may begin to look forward to eating with other family members. Try to avoid arguments during mealtimes. Explain to your child how good it is to eat together and ask them to stay at the table until everyone has finished eating.

558 A STORY ON THEIR PLATE

Why not think about renaming some of your child's least favourite foods? Turn raisins into flies, broccoli into trees, quiche into omelette cake, noodles into worms. You'll be amazed how attractive they suddenly become.

559 MAKE MEALTIME FUN

Try to create an enjoyable meal environment for your family. Don't tell them off or lecture them on anything, complain about how hard you worked to make the meal or argue with other adults. Keep conversations light and fun and let everyone contribute.

560 SIT DOWN TO EAT

Whenever possible, try to sit down with your child when they are eating, whatever age they are. If you don't want a full meal, cut up some fruit or nibble on a piece of toast and a cup of tea, so they see you eat too.

561 DON'T SNACK YOUR KIDS

If your child has a real problem with snacking and is always on at you to give them snacks, try simply not buying them for a while. If there's nothing on the shelves, you won't be able to give in to their whining!

562 KEEP THINGS HIDDEN

Don't keep snacks like crisps (chips), cookies, chocolate and sweets (candy) where children can find them and help themselves. It's fine to keep fruit, cheese and healthy snacks within reach, but make sure you are in control of their unhealthy intake.

563 GO WITH REAL DISLIKES

If your child genuinely dislikes a food, they won't be able to hide their reaction and it will show on their face immediately. Encourage them to try it again, but if you believe they honestly don't like something, don't force the issue – make them something else instead.

564 BIN THE BRIBES

Don't use snacks regularly as a way to bribe your child into good behaviour. If they get used to the idea that if they behave well you'll give them a snack, they're likely to start requesting a snack every time they do something good.

565 IN TODAY, OUT TOMORROW

It's common for pre-schoolers to take a sudden dislike to certain foods (or cups, plates, forks, you name it!). Try not to overreact to the fad of the moment. Let them eat what they want of the rest of their meal and don't believe they genuinely don't like a certain food unless they repeatedly reject it.

566 NIP IT IN THE BUD

It's much more difficult to deal with fussy or faddy eating once patterns are established than to nip it in the bud when it first begins. Children are often resistant to change so try not to let bad eating habits develop in the first place. Avoid transferring your own negative food issues to them.

567 LET THEM EAT PANCAKES

There are few things children enjoy more than helping to make pancakes, especially if it's not at a normal mealtime. Make up a batch of batter, pile some fillings onto the table and have a family pancake day.

568 PORTION CONTROL

A young child's stomach is roughly the size of their clenched fist, so bear that in mind when you're filling their plate. Give them small portions at first and then offer second helpings if they ask for more.

569 MAKE CALORIES COUNT

If your child barely eats, try to feed them nutritious but higher-calorie foods in small amounts. Instead of low-calorie 'empty' foods, try pasta, avocado, eggs, fish, sweet potatoes, peanut butter and yogurt – all are all rich in nutrients.

570 GROW YOUR OWN

If you've got space in your garden, turn your child into a vegetable lover by helping them to grow their own food. Even if you haven't got outside space, pots of herbs or tomatoes on a balcony or windowsill can help get them interested.

571 FIND A NEW FORM

Children have sensitive mouths and that goes for texture as well as taste. Sometimes they'll reject a food on the basis of the way it feels rather than the way it tastes. Offer the food in several different forms before you conclude they don't like it.

572 FEET ON THE GROUND

People are more likely to stay sitting still for longer if their feet are touching the ground, and this is the same for children. Get them a booster chair with a footrest or let them eat at a child-sized chair and table so they are able to sit still for longer.

573 SAVE THE PRAISE

Try to avoid praising your child for eating second helpings or finishing their plate. Save praise for the way they eat – using their spoon, not dropping food on the floor, etc – so that they don't associate eating too much with behaving well.

money matters

574 THINK ABOUT IT

Don't say 'yes' unless you mean it. If your child asks you if they can have something and you feel put on the spot, tell them you will think about it so you can give them a final answer rather than break a promise, which can be hard for a child to understand.

575 SECOND-HAND SAVINGS

Don't forget the second-hand option for expensive toys like tricycles, bikes, scooters, playhouses and things you might not otherwise be able to afford. Local retailers, online marketplaces like eBay, and local papers are all options.

576 KEEP TREATS SPECIAL

Try to get out of the habit of buying something for your kids every time you go out, and make treats special. If you know your child will want a new toy or a snack, take something that you already have along with you to distract them. They will soon learn not to expect something new every time they go out.

playing around

577 SAVE YOUR BLUSHES

Don't limit your child's play by being embarrassed about what you might look like as you join in their games. Children don't feel embarrassed and it's great for their development if you can take the same attitude.

578 WRITE A LIST

Create a 'rainy day' list for your kids with a list of activities they can choose from the next time it's pouring with rain. Things like making cards and painting, cooking, writing and performing a play, and so on are great indoor time fillers.

Brushes

WHITE

Blue

Red

579 INDOOR ACTIVITY

Don't limit physical play to outdoors. If it's raining and your kids need to expel some energy, make a den out of cushions and sheets in the lounge, turn the bed into a boat or play a physical game like balloon volleyball.

580 A BALANCE APPROACH

If you're going to choose one sport for your pre-schooler to try out, make it gymnastics. Because it involves so much balance and coordination, gymnastics has been shown to boost mental as well as physical development once children get to school.

581 MAKE YOUR OWN PLAYDOUGH

Make a fruit-scented playdough by combining 2 cups plain (all-purpose) flour, 4 tsp cream of tartar, 1 cup salt and 2 tbsp oil. Add to 1.5 cups of water and a sachet of fruit-flavoured drink powder, then microwave on high for 3–5 minutes, stirring every minute, until very thick. Knead until smooth and keep in an airtight container. It will keep for up to one month.

582 NURTURE IMAGINATION

Most children enjoy believing in such make-believe characters as Santa Claus, fairies, goblins, wizards and witches. Don't worry that their beliefs aren't realistic – studies show it's healthy for children to use their imagination.

583 PLAY MAGIC CARPETS

A great game for your child's imagination is the magic carpet. Lay a rug or blanket on the floor and sit on it with your child. Ask them where they want to travel to and help them tell stories and think of new things to say about it.

584 BREAK IT UP

Try to avoid buying expensive, breakable toys and ornaments for children and if they receive them as gifts, keep them out of reach until you're there to supervise. Otherwise, you'll constantly be telling them to be careful, which isn't exactly conducive to a fun play session!

585 BE FANTASTIC

Play a fantasy game with your child by asking them what they want to be when they grow up. It's a great way to explore their imagination. Ask them questions about what they would do if they grew up to be a firefighter, dancer, doctor, etc.

586 MAKE UP A STORY

Don't feel you always have to read your child a book. You could make up a story instead, using your child's name as the hero or heroine. Run the story over several nights and let them help you come up with new ideas.

time for yourself

587 TAKE TURNS FOR TIME OFF

If you have another adult in your family, take turns getting away. Alternate weekend lie-ins and try and each have a night away with friends or alone every few months. If you're a single parent, ask friends and relatives to help.

588 BE GOOD TO YOURSELF

To be a good parent you have to take care of yourself, particularly during the early years. As parents you are often exhausted and may have other worries such as jobs, money and various other life issues. If you feel overwhelmed, tell someone and get some help.

589 SHARE THE SHOPPING

Is there anyone who can look after the kids when you go shopping? Although there is not always a babysitter to hand when you want to go shopping, there may be times when you can share babysitting with friends so that you can avoid the stress of shopping with the children.

590 TIME OUT

If you feel bogged down by family life, try and make time for yourself in small ways. Make a deal with the kids – a trip to the park in exchange for 5 minutes of peace and quiet where you can have a cup of tea or a chat with your friend.

591 KNOW YOUR WEAKNESSES

Recognize the issues you find difficult to deal with and ask others for help. For instance, if your children's cheekiness or lack of appetite pushes your buttons, ask your partner, another carer or grandparent to take control of those issues.

592 SHOP FROM YOUR SOFA

Online shopping is a real bonus for working parents, who now have a way of avoiding the weekend rush with unwilling children in tow. Even clothes can be bought online as most stores have good return policies, and toys are often cheaper as well.

593 SINGLE SAVIOURS

If you're a single parent ask a parent, sibling or close friend for some relief from the incessant responsibility of early childcare. Their help, even one or two nights a week, can give you some rest. Don't be afraid to ask for support.

594 CHOOSE QUANTITY NOT QUALITY

Don't worry about making sure every second you spend with your children is quality time because it's important for them to experience the reality of life. Instead, concentrate on spending as much time with them as you can.

FINDING THEIR FEET

keeping the peace

595 GO WITH YOUR GUT FEELING

If someone or something makes you feel uncomfortable, go with your gut feeling. Teach your children to trust their instincts too, by listening to them and respecting what they feel.

596 REALLY MEAN IT

Children may push your limits but often they do this to see how firm and secure their world is; saying 'no' may really be what they want and need. Don't make threats you can't carry out, as this will just encourage them to keep pushing to find the real boundary.

597 DON'T BURDEN THEM

Don't demand or expect constant love and affection from your children or ask them if they love you, especially if you are feeling low and your children know it. Expectations like this can lead to feelings of guilt and depression in the long term.

598 DON'T JUMP IN

Resist the temptation to answer your child too quickly if they're talking about their feelings. Adult brains work quicker than children's, so limiting your responses to 'mmmh' and 'I see' until you are sure they've finished gives them space for further thought and discussion.

599 THINK AHEAD

Use positive phrases to help your pre-teen learn to tidy up. Instead of nagging them about leaving their stuff lying around, involve them by saying, 'Where do you want to store your trainers so you can find them again easily?'

600 REAP THE REWARDS

Rewards should be earned rather than given, but they don't have to be sweets (candy) or chocolate. Try rewarding good behaviour with a trip to the park, a game of your child's choosing, some dancing, singing or cooking. Give the reward as soon as possible – the longer you wait, the weaker the association between behaviour and reward.

601 SAY NO TO NAGGING

Try to avoid the urge to nag your children, especially as they get older. Pre-teens whose parents always nag them to finish tasks are less likely to learn to take responsibility for themselves, which in turn makes them dependent on the nagging.

602 CUT THE REPETITION

When your child is a toddler you'll get used to telling them the same thing a thousand times a day. But as they get older, don't fall into the trap of continuing this. For a pre-teen repeating is nagging, so phase it out by the time your child is ten or eleven.

603 TURN OFF THE BOX

Make a family pact to watch less television. The key to reducing resistance to this is to allocate one 'no TV' evening a week and take turns in choosing what to do instead. It shouldn't always be you who suggests the alternative. Let them decide, and spend some quality time together.

604 WITHDRAW A PRIVILEGE

If your child is over five and resists going to time out, add on extra minutes for resistance, and stick to your timings. If they still refuse to go, use withdrawal of privileges such as TV watching.

stay calm

605 CHANGE YOUR BEHAVIOUR

You can't change your child, only the way they behave. And it's the same for you – don't feel you have to change your beliefs in order to change your behaviour. It's possible to act calm and unconcerned even when you're seething inside.

606 DON'T GENERALIZE

When people are angry, it's common for them to exaggerate their feelings. Try to avoid using expressions like, 'you always', or 'you never' when you're talking to your children as they are likely to become defensive. Make sure that what you accuse them of is specific – and true!

607 PASS ON YOUR MESSAGE

Think about the behaviours and messages you want to pass on to your kids. Write up a 'wisdom' list with all the qualities you'd like to see your children develop and think about how you can model and teach them.

608 NOBODY'S PERFECT

Remember it's impossible to be a perfect parent, even if you try your very best. Allow yourself some limitations, don't be afraid to admit them to others and don't put pressure on yourself to get everything right.

609 CALM HELPS

If two people are angry or lose their tempers and begin to shout at each other, the argument is unlikely to be solved. If you stay calm, your child is more likely to copy you and it's more likely you'll resolve differences.

610 AVOID THE 'BUT'

It's natural you to want to help your child become better but avoid using phrases like, 'it's very good, but…' Your child is more likely to remember the 'but' than the initial praise.

611 BE A ROLE MODEL

Be a role model for your children but don't make it obvious you are setting yourself up as an example. For instance, 'I don't feel like clearing up now but it has to be done, so I'd better get on with it.' Just say and do it, without meaningful looks in their direction.

612 SPACE TO GROW

Show respect for their opinions even if you disagree. Don't try to change them into something you want them to be. A useful trick is to imagine they were someone else's child and ask yourself, 'Would I say that if it wasn't my son or daughter?' If the answer is 'no', then bite your tongue.

613 ACCEPT THEIR CHOICES

Accept your children for what they are. Don't comment negatively on their clothes, music or taste in television – pop culture has filtered down to the school playground! At the same time, there's nothing wrong with 'babyish' activities; children develop at their own pace.

614 PICK YOUR BATTLES

If you say 'no' to everything, your child is likely to start rebelling against everything! Give them some credit. If your son is doing well at school, does it matter if he stays up later at weekends? If your daughter dresses herself well, why can't she wear wellies in the summer?

615 JUST ENOUGH

The most effective praise has been shown to be when you just let them know you are pleased and leave it at that. If you are trying to foster good behaviour in your child, praise them appropriately but don't go overboard, and try to avoid comparing the good behaviour to what they would 'usually' do.

616 PRAISE ALL ROUND

Encourage your child to praise their siblings and friends as well as giving them praise yourself. That way, they will start to make the link between offering praise and receiving it, and will learn to appreciate the actions of others.

617 PILE OFF THE PRESSURE

Be careful about how you praise your child. Saying things like 'you're always kind' could cause your child to feel concerned they don't deserve the praise. Make sure you praise specific events and actions rather than offering general praise.

618 DON'T SAY 'I TOLD YOU SO'

As your child gets older, they are likely to develop a strong dislike of being wrong! Don't worry, this is only natural for pre-teens. Don't remind them every time you were right – let them find things out for themselves.

playing for time

619 PLAY AROUND

Play brings you closer to your children. It also helps them to become more independent, teaches them to problem solve and to cooperate with others by working in teams. It develops concentration, coordination and imagination, all key skills for school and learning.

620 BAKE BREAD

Why not make some bread with your child? This is a great idea if they have friends round, as you can combine an activity with making their own lunch!

621 USE YOUR UTENSILS

Remember that when your younger kids are playing with playdough or modelling clay, your kitchen implements and gadgets can be great fun – garlic presses, pizza cutters, potato mashers and cookie cutters are all good fun choices.

622 MIX UP THE PAINTS

Mixing in a squirt of washing-up liquid to your child's poster paints will make it much easier to wash them out of clothes and wipe off surfaces because it stops them sticking so hard in the first place.

623 KEEP CONTAINERS

Don't throw away containers/jars/boxes. Use them to store crayons, pastels, chalk, glitter and so on.

624 TRY SPYING

A useful indoor game that will keep your older children occupied if the weather is bad is to play 'spies' with them. Write with invisible ink, create 'mirror writing' letters and even make and break your own codes.

625 A PLACE TO PAINT

Try to avoid having art supplies within easy reach of your child until they are old enough to supervise themselves. Instead, keep them apart from other toys until they are used, then choose a convenient place, like the kitchen table, where you can keep an eye on them.

creating confidence

626 FIND YOUR CHILD'S TALENTS

Every child has a natural collection of skills and talents, and by exposing them to as many different experiences as you can, you will help to unlock their interests and skills, which in turn promotes confidence and allows them to reach their potential. Let them try out various music, sport or creative activities, and don't worry if they fail or become disenchanted. Once they find something they really love doing, they will stick with it.

627 LOVE EACH OTHER

One of the most powerful influences on children's sexual identity and confidence is the way they perceive the adult relationships in their home. If their parents or carers are loving and supportive towards each other, they are more likely to form healthy relationships themselves.

628 MUSICALLY EDUCATED

Scientists say that children who are exposed to music or those who play an instrument do better in school than those who don't. Music can benefit a child's reading age, IQ and the development of certain parts of the brain. It teaches discipline and can relieve stress.

629 HOLD ON TO HUGS

Studies have shown that children who experience physical affection from their parents or carers – such as hugging, hand-holding, etc – feel more secure and settled as adults and are more comfortable in relationships. Be affectionate with your child and frequently tell them you love them.

630 SPEND TIME IN THEIR ROOM

If your child has problems sleeping or staying in their room at night, it might be because they associate it with being alone. Spend more time with them in their room in the daytime, and make it comfortable with toys and books they enjoy.

631 LET'S TALK ABOUT SEX

Pre-teens are notorious for being misinformed about sex. If you haven't already explained to your pre-teen where babies come from, now is the time, as they will most likely have heard it from their friends at school. You may need to find out what information they already have before you give them the truth.

632 CHAMPION YOUR CHILD

Praise talents and achievements instead of using sarcasm to point out weaknesses.

Be positive and encouraging and never ignore good behaviour, as there is then no incentive for your child to repeat it. Be encouraging of all of his or her successes, no matter how small, and keep it up for life! Children never outgrow the need to hear praise from their parents.

633 DON'T COMPARE THEM

Make sure you avoid talking about your children in front of others, particularly when it comes to describing the differences between them. Comparing siblings almost always leads to bad feeling for one or both, so avoid it completely to be safe.

634 PRAISE THE ACTION

Instead of praising or criticizing your child directly – for instance, by saying, 'you're clever', or 'you're naughty' – link the words to a specific action, like 'it was naughty of you to…' etc. This will help keep their self-esteem high.

635 TELL THEM THEY'RE GOOD

It's natural for children to say things like 'I'm no good at football' or 'I can't draw properly' if they've seen adults or other children doing better. Reassure your child they are good and make sure they know your love isn't conditional on their abilities.

636 SPILL YOUR BELIEFS

Remember to bring up the fact that open communication with you about sex does not in any way imply that you condone sexual behaviour at their age. This will clear any confusion your pre-teen may have and calm some of your own concerns. If they ask, don't be afraid to tell them about your beliefs.

637 DAD'S AND DAUGHTERS

It's well-known how important a father's input is into their sons' development, but it's just as important to daughters. Studies have shown that a woman's confidence is greatly affected by her relationship with her father, so don't neglect your daughter.

638 TELL HIM YOU LOVE HIM

Telling your son you love him won't spoil him; it will make a man out of him. When it comes to fathers and sons, the important thing is that sons see their dads as strong and healthy role models who are capable of exhibiting love and showing feelings, so don't hold back.

639 BODY CONFIDENCE

Talking about sex and relationships with your pre-teen goes hand in hand with talking about their own body image and self-worth. All too often, these issues are tied together in young people's minds, and it's up to you to help untangle them.

640 DON'T FORGET DAD

Psychologists have shown that although the mother is the centre of many families, it is the child's relationship with their father that will model their adult sexual behaviour and confidence at relationship building. Make sure dad is involved too (or another male adult).

641 KEEP IT LIGHT

The best thing for your pre-teen is to talk to both parents about sex, but not together. If you feel uncomfortable, that's okay. The likelihood is that your pre-teen feels a lot more so. Try to keep conversations light and with some humour.

action stations

642 AGE APPROPRIATE

Children under five should explore how to run, jump and tumble on their own. From six to eight, most kids are ready to take on an organized sport with an emphasis on skills, not competition. From nine to twelve, they are ready to start combining skills. Work with your child to get the level right.

643 GET INVOLVED

Reports have shown that children who see their parents taking part in sport or activities are far more likely to get involved themselves. Give them the message that activity is a lifelong habit by getting active yourself.

644 START AT THE RIGHT LEVEL

Make sure you don't set your kids up for a fall by trying to jump the gun in sports classes. Make sure they join at a level that's appropriate to their skill – even if their friends are in another group – so they aren't embarrassed or teased.

645 LET THEM DECIDE

Once your child reaches eight or nine years old, they have a good idea of what they do and don't like. Get them involved in making decisions about what sports they do regularly and what outings they want to go on.

646 MAKE IT INDIVIDUAL

Avoid the temptation to encourage your child to take up a particular sport because the club happens to be nearby, all your neighbours are signing up their kids or because you were good at it when you were young. Instead, help your child find a sport that fits their personality.

647 TEAM UP FOR TEAMWORK

Getting your child involved in team sports won't just teach them about working together and give them some exercise. Sport also provides a great opportunity for kids to learn about disappointment and failure, as well as how to win and lose gracefully – all good life skills.

648 HELP THEM CROSS-TRAIN

Helping your children enjoy activity is one of the best and healthiest habits you can help them develop. However, try to avoid concentrating on just one sport while they are still growing (which carries on well into their teens) as this can increase their chances of injury and burn-out.

649 OFFER ALTERNATIVES

If your child doesn't enjoy school sports because of the competitive element, see if they enjoy alternative activities like ballet, yoga, cycling, rock climbing, gymnastics or martial arts instead. Often, non-sporty kids just need to find something they enjoy.

650 NO GAIN FROM PAIN

Let your child know they should never continue playing sport if they are in pain. Make sure they understand that untreated injuries could mean they have to stay inactive for longer to heal.

651 STAY ACTIVE ALL YEAR

Something like a quarter of childhood injuries seen in hospital emergency departments are due to sporting accidents, many at the beginning of the season following a prolonged rest. Help your child to minimize their chances of injury by encouraging them to stay active in the off-season.

652 INVOLVE THEM

If your child prefers watching sport to doing it, try to involve them in activities that are similar to their favourite sports and get into the spirit with them. Buy them a punchbag, or basketball hoop, or go down to the park with them and kick a ball around. They may find they enjoy a more relaxed and non-competitive approach to their favourite sport.

653 SET AN EXAMPLE

Help your child learn good sportsmanship by setting them a good example, both from the sidelines and when you play. Don't criticize other players, referees or coaches in front of them, and teach them to show grace in victory and good humour in defeat.

654 STICK TO THEIR PACE

Be careful of jumping on your child's sports' bandwagon and encouraging their coach to move them up a level before they are ready. The decision to move up should come from the child themselves (and their coach) if it's going to work most effectively.

655 YOUR OWN SPORTS DAY

If you're looking after other children and the house is getting crowded, why not get them outside into the park or garden for a mini sports day? Soft balls, skipping ropes and a couple good trees to climb are all you need for a whole day's fun.

656 HOLD BACK

Don't try and 'push' your kids into learning skills too early. Experts say that children develop motor skills individually, so what's true for one child may not be for another. As long as your children are active, early training has little effect on development.

657 USE DISTRACTION TACTICS

A day out having fun at a theme park or even in the park with mum and dad can make a child forget they're upset over falling out with a friend. Joining a new drama or gymnastics group can soften the blow of not making it onto the football team.

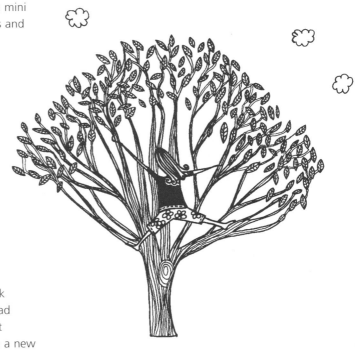

658 PICNIC PREP

Taking your kids for a picnic on a sunny day can be a great way of getting them out in the fresh air. Why not turn it into a challenge by buying ingredients then letting them prepare the picnic in the morning?

bad habits

659 STOP THE BAD HABITS

Habits like thumb-sucking and nail-biting that are cute in little children can become irritating in older children. Help your child get over their habit by giving them a diversion habit (like squeezing a ball or flicking a wristband). You could even try offering an incentive (or treat) to stop.

660 IGNORE IRRITATIONS

Don't worry if your child has habits (like twitching) that you don't like or find unattractive. As long as they're not causing your child problems, it's often best to leave them to grow out of it. Don't draw attention to it and try not to worry.

661 DON'T REACT TO SWEARING

Even very young children understand shock value, and the more the audience reacts to a 'naughty' word, the more likely they are to repeat it. Try not to react with shock or surprise, and calmly tell your child that swearing is not acceptable.

coping with change

662 TEACH THEM TO TALK

You can't wave a magic wand and vanish away a child's unhappy feelings. What you can do is help them to learn how to manage what they do about them. Encourage them to tell you how they feel by saying, 'I feel angry/ left out/put down'.

663 REVIEW THE RULES

Be age and stage appropriate in the rules you set for your children – what is OK for a 9-year-old will be restricting for an 11-year-old. Make sure you review your house rules regularly and involve your children in deciding what's fair.

664 SHOW YOUR LOVE

It isn't easy loving or showing affection for a child who is being angry or hurtful, but they need to be shown that they are acceptable even if their actions aren't. Separate who they are from what they do by saying, 'I love you but I don't love what you're doing'.

665 KEEP IN TOUCH ON TRIPS

As your child gets older, the safety issue becomes more important. They might start going to sleepovers and school trips where they'll be out of your direct control. It's important to communicate – with them, the school, their friends and other parents – so you stay in the loop.

666 TAKE A WORK TRIP

If your pre-teen complains about you or your partner working all the time, try taking them to work with you for a day or so. Knowing what you do while you're out of the house will help them to feel involved and cope better with your absences.

667 BALANCE YOUR LIFE

Many fathers prioritize providing – through work – over family time. This is understandable, but make sure you don't fall into the trap of providing for a family you never see. Seek a balance between work and home time.

668 WEBCAM COMMUNICATION

If you or your partner have to travel a lot for work, consider investing in a webcam so you can speak directly to your child while you are away. Children respond better to absence if they know they are being thought about so remind them you miss them.

669 TRUST THEIR INSTINCTS

One of the best ways to help your child stay safe, especially when you're not around, is to have confidence in them and let them know it. Give them appropriate responsibility for their age, such as walking to school or taking a bus ride on their own, and prepare them well. Trusting them is a way of teaching them to be responsible.

schooldays

670 DON'T BAN FRIENDS

If you're worried about your child getting in with a 'bad' crowd, don't make the mistake of trying to ban them from seeing friends. Instead, try to set realistic rules, like supervising time together or inviting them to your house so you can keep an eye on them.

671 SNACK THEM UP FOR HOMEWORK

Children are often hungry when they come home from school, and they're unlikely to be able to concentrate on homework if their stomachs are grumbling. Make sure they have a nutritious snack that will keep them going until dinner before they settle down to work.

672 EYE WATCH

You should get your child's sight tested regularly, but if they suddenly start performing worse at school get an eye test even if they've had one recently. This is often the age when visual problems start to show up, so be vigilant.

673 DON'T TAKE OVER

Resist the temptation to do your child's homework yourself – not only is it not fair on the rest of the class, it's not fair on your child because if you always do it for them they'll never learn how to do things for themselves.

674 BE PREPARED

Prepare in advance for the return to term time, then you won't be in a panic buying uniforms, satchels, stationery and so on at the last minute. Not only does this mean you can shop around for the best deals, but it will help reassure your child that they're ready to go back to school.

675 BE A POSITIVE PARENT

Children can pick up on parental anxieties about school – say, if you did badly at school or were bullied. Try to be positive and show children that education is important and will benefit them, even if they are unfamiliar with the language or the school system.

676 SHARE AN INTEREST

Children benefit from having both their parents showing an interest in their schooling. Parents living apart can still share this role and can ask the school to make sure information is sent to more than one address.

677 GET BACK TO NORMAL

Start finding your routine again near the end of the school holidays. Getting back to schoolday bedtimes is a good place to start, then it will not be such a shock when term starts again.

678 TALK ABOUT CHANGE

Whether it is a new school or a change in your family's circumstances, make time to talk about any fears or worries with your children, and do what you can to minimize anxiety – like doing a 'dry run' to the school.

679 KEEP THEM IN THE LOOP

Your child may be worried about losing friends who are going to a different school. You could try inviting an old school friend round for dinner at the end of the first week so they can compare notes and reassure each other they haven't lost contact.

680 DON'T IGNORE ISSUES

Readdress any problems left over from the previous term. If your child has experienced bullying or has had problems at school, make sure you understand what they want to happen when the next term starts, even if this just means talking about it.

681 PLAN THEIR EDUCATION

If you want your child to go on to further education like university or college, it's worth thinking about how you're going to fund this while they're still quite young.

682 LOUD TO BE PROUD

If your child is about to start an important year at school they will need a bit more reassurance in the lead up to the new school year. Make sure you show you are proud of them.

683 NOT ALONE

If your child is worried about starting a new school, remind them that everyone is in the same position and even if other children don't seem nervous, they probably are. Try to be there for them in the first few weeks so they can discuss things with you. Keep it low-key and avoid too many questions if they aren't forthcoming – they'll talk to you in their own time.

684 LET THEM WORK IT OUT

If your child is doing their schoolwork, try not to interfere too much with how they do it. Some children need a break after school whereas others like to get home and do their homework straight away. Unless they're struggling, try to let them find their own path.

685 CUT THEM SOME SLACK

Be prepared to give them a bit of leeway for the first week after the school holidays. School can be a long day for kids and when they are out of practice it can be exhausting. Make sure they are well-fed and rested, and go easy on routines for a while.

keeping them occupied

686 ON THE FARM

If you're stuck for what to do with your children at the weekend or during the school holidays, why not visit a farm? Even many cities now have farms where children can feed the animals and play a variety of games.

687 A LITTLE SQUIRT

To liven things up in the paddling pool, rinse out old squeezy bottles and let the kids squirt each other, or let them play with bubbles. Make sure you keep an eye on children when water is around, but try to let them play without your interference.

688 DOWN MEMORY LANE

When your child reaches around seven or eight years of age, they will probably start to get interested in what they used to be like when they were smaller. Why not use up a rainy afternoon to make up a 'memory' book that includes pictures of them growing up? Talk about the photos as you select them.

689 VISIT A GALLERY

As your child gets older, they will enjoy doing more 'adult' things in their school holidays like going to museums or art galleries (many of which are free) and to concerts or the theatre. Keep these visits short to begin with as your child will probably become very tired.

690 GIVE THEM A TASK

If you've got more than one child to keep occupied during the school holidays, it can seem daunting. Get them to work together by giving them a theme and getting them to come up with a play, story or dance routine.

691 CHECK OUT FREE ACTIVITIES

Make sure you contact your local council and other organizations about holiday activities. Many places now offer free or subsidized sports and craft activities for children.

692 BEDROOM MAKEOVER

Once every few years, help your child to give their room a mini makeover with posters, paint and maybe some new furniture. Let them think about what colour scheme they want and help them plan how to make changes.

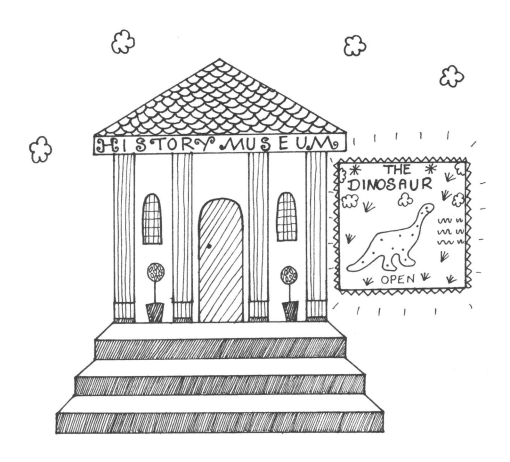

693 CAMP OUT

Why not take your kids camping for a night? Children find camping out really good fun and you don't have to travel miles – a tent in the backyard can be just as exciting!

pester power

694 'NO' MEANS 'NO'

Teaching your children the value of money is an extremely good lesson. When you say 'no' to a new toy or clothes, mean it. If your kids know that you will eventually cave in, they will keep trying.

695 GIVE YOUR REASONS

When you say 'no' to buying a new toy or gadget, it may help to talk to your child about why; 'because I say so' is not enough for your child to understand. But be firm, so you don't get caught in the trap of haggling or arguing.

696 HOLD ON TO YOUR PURSE STRINGS

Don't feel guilty about not having the money to give in to 'pester power'. Nobody has a bottomless purse, but it can be hard when you can't afford to give your children the things you want to. It helps to be honest and explain what is value for money and affordable.

697 GIFT TIMES

Try to involve your child in choosing Christmas and birthday presents, both for themselves and for other members of the family. Present-buying is a great way to help them learn about the value of money, and buying good presents is a great skill!

698 THINGS THAT MATTER

Even if you say no to a new purchase, try to show your child you understand how they feel. Sometimes we forget how important something as simple as a pair of trainers (sneakers) or the latest football shirt or gadget can be. Always try not to be flippant with their feelings.

699 SHORTEN THE LIST

Remember that children change their minds every week with new crazes. Help them see they can't have everything they want and if it is a Christmas list, tell them that not even Santa Claus has that much money. Ask them to list presents in order of preference, with a limit of five.

700 OPEN AN ACCOUNT

It's a good idea to open a bank account for your child as soon as possible to help them understand the concept of saving money and being responsible. Most banks now have childhood schemes specifically designed for different ages.

701 INVEST FOR THE FUTURE

In some countries there are tax-free savings and investment plans for children under the ages of 16 or 18. Take advantage of these financial plans to help your child understand the importance of saving for the future.

mealtime madness

702 FILL UP ON PROTEIN

If your child has decided to become a vegetarian, make sure they get enough protein (from eggs, dairy products, beans, fish) and that their iron levels are topped up with green vegetables, fortified breakfast cereals or a supplement.

703 SHELVE YOUR SNACKS

Why not give your children their own shelf in the fridge from which they can help themselves to healthy snacks? Keep it full of chopped fruit, vegetable sticks, cheese and other treats.

704 SAY CHEERS TO CHEESE

Cheese is a great snack food because it contains both protein and fat, which means even a small amount of it is filling enough to take away hunger pangs but it's not bulky enough to ruin the appetite for the next meal. It also contains high levels of calcium.

705 IRON OUT TIREDNESS

Iron deficiency is a common problem in young people, and two of the main symptoms are tiredness and lack of concentration. If you notice these in your child, try to make sure they have enough iron (found in fortified cereals, red meat and green vegetables).

706 KEEP HUNGER AT BAY

Getting your child to eat healthy snacks can be hard, but they are less likely to be fussy if they are really hungry. After school is a great time to go for healthy snacks, as they often come home starving – try fresh fruit, vegetables with hummus, wraps or sandwiches.

HUMMUS

708 LET THEM GO HUNGRY

Food can often be a real battleground, with children latching on to their parent's emotional need to feed and nurture. If your child refuses to eat a meal, avoid the temptation to let them fill up on unhealthy snacks between meals. It might not do them any harm to go hungry for a while and they are more likely to eat the next time.

709 DO A BLIND TASTING

If your child is becoming increasingly fussy, try turning tasting new foods into a game. Use a blindfold and hold a quiz with all your children and see if they can identify certain tastes, then allow them to do the same to you (within reason!). They'll soon forget their resistance.

710 SNACKED OUT

Children often find it difficult to get enough energy from just three meals a day, so offer snacks in the morning and afternoon. Fruit or cheese are better than cookies and cake because they are healthier and your child is less likely to want them instead of their next meal.

707 LUNCHBOX WARS

It's almost impossible to control your children's eating when you're not with them, and lunchtimes at school can be difficult, especially if their friends are taking junk foods. Try to get the school to set some rules on packed lunches – such as no fizzy drinks and limited crisps (chips) – to make it easier for everyone.

711 OIL THEIR MINDS

Omega-3 oils are great for your child's growth, helping their mental and physical development as well as concentration and performance at school. Try to include two or three portions of fish per week in their diet (sardines, salmon and mackerel are best) or use a supplement.

712 LET THEM HELP YOU

The time just before dinner is often fraught with problems – children are hungry and often tired and you're in the kitchen preparing food. If this is a difficult time for your family, take their minds off the conflict by involving them in laying the table or preparing food.

713 THE RIGHT RULES

Set 'table rules' for family mealtimes but make them appropriate. Rules like 'no TV while you're eating' are applicable to any age, but staying at the table until everyone has finished eating or saying 'please' and 'thank you' are particularly important to teach to older children.

714 KEEP PORTIONS SMALL

Don't put your child off by putting too much food on their plate to start with. It's better to give them second helpings than make them feel daunted by a piled plate. One tablespoon of each food for each year of their age is a rough guideline.

715 EAT TOGETHER

Make it your family's aim to eat at least one meal a day together if it's possible (it doesn't matter if it's breakfast). If not, make sure you make time at the weekends for family meals where everyone sits at the table together.

relax & unwind

716 CREATE SPACE

If you've got limited space in your family home and everyone doesn't have their own room, you can still create space for your children to call their own. Invest in a wigwam or playhouse that they can make into their own private space, or convert a garden shed into a games room.

717 CHILLED KIDS

Help your child learn relaxation. Get them to breathe in for two seconds and out for three or four, continuing in that rhythm, to reduce stress and anxiety. They can use this technique to relax in bed or calm themselves before tests and exams.

718 THINK HAPPY PLACES

It's difficult to be stressed if you're thinking of something enjoyable, so if your child has trouble relaxing, teach them a basic meditation technique by getting them to close their eyes and imagine a 'happy' place – often, this is somewhere they remember from a holiday or some other time they felt totally relaxed.

719 CLENCH AND UNCLENCH

Sometimes, not being able to sleep at night is due to tensions held in the body. Help your child to relax by getting them to clench the muscles in their feet for a few seconds, then release. Work over their whole body, ending with the head and face, for total body relaxation.

720 GIVE THEM SOME TIME

Make sure your child has enough time to relax and do nothing – it's important for children to have time alone and space to think. Rushing them from one lesson or 'improving' activity to another might seem good for their development, but downtime is important too.

sticky issues

721 TAKE AWAY LOOT

If you find your child stealing, don't allow them to profit from wrongdoing – return any stolen object. Teach your child about money – give pocket money in return for chores (such as folding washing) as this will help them appreciate that money is earned. Don't leave cash lying around if you know it will tempt them.

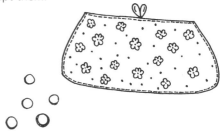

722 DON'T OVERREACT

The first time your child does something wrong, make sure your reactions aren't too harsh. The fear of punishment can turn a child into a habitual liar and they must be able to trust you. Let them know what they have done is wrong and if it happens again they will be punished.

723 ALLOW THE FANTASIES

At the younger end of this age group, children begin to understand the difference between fact and fiction. A six-year-old knows they're not really in a spaceship when they play at going to the moon. However, it's sometimes easier for them to go back to fantasies that worked well when they were younger, particularly to avoid unpleasant experiences.

724 PRIVATE EXPLORATION

It's perfectly reasonable for children of seven or eight to become interested in exploring their private parts. Don't react to this with disgust, worry about what it means or tell them it's wrong. Simply let them know that touching private parts of our body is something we do in private, not in front of other people.

725 USE DISTRACTION

Most of the touching and exploring that goes on between children is part of a game. If you see this kind of play, distract them by asking them to put their clothes back on and do something else. Make sure they know that some parts of their body are private and no one else may touch.

726 STOP AND THINK

Think carefully before you accuse your child of lying. It's only from about seven to eight years of age that children can fully understand the difference between truth and lies. Before that they're not 'lying' in the adult sense, as they may genuinely believe they saw a fairy in the garden!

727 BE THERE IF THEY NEED YOU

Becoming independent is the main preoccupation of your pre-teen child and you might often feel rejected. But despite their mixed feelings about you, they still need your love and support with no strings attached. Don't force them to give you hugs or kisses, but be there with support if they need it.

728 TALK TO THEIR TEACHER

If your child finds it hard making friends at school, don't be afraid to enlist the help of their teacher – they might be able to help by changing seating arrangements around or suggesting children who might have similar interests.

729 DON'T TAKE OFFENCE

As your pre-teen develops, their relationship with you becomes more complicated. They still need you, but probably wish they didn't. Expect that at some point you will be an embarrassment to your child but it's impossible to predict in what way. Don't take it personally if they criticize you; just try to stay calm and wait for it to pass.

730 TAKE MATTERS SERIOUSLY

Take your child's problems and dilemmas seriously. You may feel your pre-teen's latest worry is trivial but to them it's a matter of life and death, so listen and answer carefully. Don't tell your child's worries to other people without their permission, which could cause them not to trust you.

maintaining relationships

731 SYMPATHIZE AND EMPATHIZE
Even teenagers who have been caring children are likely to lose the ability to empathize at some point in their teens. Remind them that their actions have consequences but don't blame them. Explain your feelings using phrases like 'when you did that, it made me feel…'

732 HAVE A REUNION
Often, parents with teenagers seldom see their children. Make a chart for the walls of your hall or kitchen where every family member is expected to write where they are and when they're due back (and that includes you).

733 BEND THE RULES
Teenage years are a real mix between rules and responsibilities. It's important that you set rules and are consistent, but it's also important not to be too didactic – have regular discussions about the rules and be prepared to give and take a bit.

734 EXPECT THE BEST

Teenagers tend to live up, or down, to your expectations. The more positive, loving, respectful and affirming you are, the more they will respond and listen to you. Being the parent of a teenager is hard work, but take time for yourself and try to be positive towards them.

735 BE GENEROUS

Although teenagers may appear to not want attention, they often crave it more than when they were younger. They may behave badly as a way of getting attention from their parents. Let them know you love them and try to praise them for the things they have done well.

736 TALK ABOUT FRIENDS

A good way to teach your teenager some emotional intelligence is to allow them to discuss with you the problems and issues their friends (and your friends) are having. Often, teenagers won't want to talk about their own feelings but will be keen to talk about their friends.

737 GIVE GOOD PRAISE

If your teenager does something you like, make sure they understand what they are being praised for. Show approval, describe what they did and give the reason why it pleased you, eg, 'Thanks for phoning. I'm really glad you told me you were going to be late. Remembering to phone shows a lot of sensitivity and proves I can trust you.'

738 UNDERSTAND THEM

To help your teenager feel you understand them, suggest that once a month you do something together that they choose – it might be going to a museum that's linked to their school studies, an art gallery or just out to lunch or dinner. Try to let them lead the conversation.

739 FACE THE CHALLENGE

Teenagers often feel the need to challenge everything and that includes your rules, beliefs, thoughts and even casual comments. Try to acknowledge what they say and believe, even if you don't agree with it.

740 GIVE THEM SPACE

Changing bodies and intense feelings and thoughts can leave a teenager feeling very self-conscious, so their space and privacy is important. This is especially important when it comes to physical privacy and time with their friends. Let them have their own space to unwind, read, listen to music, talk with their friends or just be alone.

741 CHANGE YOUR PATTERNS

It's common for teenagers and their parents to come to loggerheads regularly. Keep track of your disagreements to see if they are following the same pattern. If they are, try to change your behaviour, for instance, by staying calm when you would normally shout.

742 NO LONGER A CHILD

As your child turns into a teenager, they are starting to become an adult. They'll often think they're there, even if you know they've got a long way to go. Try not to talk down to them or treat them like a child, which can be really frustrating.

743 LEND A LISTENING EAR

Nothing bugs a teenager more than sensing that their parents don't understand their viewpoint, or haven't tried to understand. Before you can get through to them, make sure you listen carefully to what they have to say and try to put yourself in their shoes.

744 WORK OUT THEIR EMOTIONS

Some teenagers – boys in particular – have a less developed range of emotional expression to call on. Embarrassment, irritation and disappointment are difficult emotions and anger is the way some teenagers express themselves. Many young men find sport or playing music are good ways to work out emotional stress.

745 BOOST THEIR CONFIDENCE

Children often hit a patch of uncertainty as they change into teenagers, where they begin to be unsure about their abilities and their confidence wanes. Try to bolster their confidence by involving them in activities they enjoy and are good at.

746 BE THERE

Round about the age of 11 or 12, your children are likely to become much more interested in what their friends think than what you think. Don't try to fight this – it's a natural progression from 'parental' to 'peer' pressure, but try to listen to their worries.

747 BE A THREE-TO-ONE PARENT

Every time you give your teenager one consequence for bad or antisocial behaviour, make an effort to also provide three opportunities for them to earn your praise, thanks or a reward.

748 FASHION VICTIMS

Support your child's choices as much as you can when it comes to fashion – remember how important it was to you when you were younger? However, talk to them seriously about long-lasting issues like piercings and tattoos, which could have an impact on their future.

749 THE WAY YOU WERE

About the time your child becomes a teenager, they are likely to become very interested in what you did, thought and believed when you were their age. Showing them photos and videos and answering questions about your own relationships, interests and feelings at that time, can help them feel you understand them better.

750 MUM NOT MATE

Try to avoid using your child as a confidante. Although they may be interested in your problems, they are probably not emotionally equipped to deal with them and it may cause them stress and anxiety. This is particularly important for single parents who don't have a partner to talk to. Call a friend or family member instead.

751 TEACH THEM SMALL TALK

Help foster good social skills in your children by encouraging them to spend time with people of all ages. Let them circulate with your friends at the beginning of parties and spend time with other families at weekends.

752 AVOID PSYCHO BABBLE

Avoid playing pop psychologist to your teenager – there's nothing more irritating to young people than a parent telling them how they feel. Instead, let them approach you and tell you how they feel when they want to, and don't probe them with constant questions.

753 LISTENING SKILLS

If your teenager approaches you to talk about something that is worrying them, try to avoid jumping in with your views or advice. Let them finish what they are saying and make yourself listen in silence to get more out of them.

754 THINK BEFORE YOU ACT

All parents know it's wrong to read their child's diary, listen to phone calls, follow them to places or check their emails, but many will do it anyway. If you are tempted to snoop into your child's private life, make sure that you think through the consequences first.

755 DON'T CAVE IN

Pick your battles with your teenager, and stick to your guns on things you feel strongly about. It probably won't work to nag them about doing something constructive with their spare time, for example, but it's fine to put down your foot about writing thank you cards for presents, etc.

756 TALK DIRECTLY

Teenagers are kings and queens of the 'don't care' shrug. Don't give them a chance to reply sullenly or to accuse you of whining at them. Ask them things directly, 'pick up your coat please' rather than 'will you please…' or 'can't you just…'

757 DON'T CRUSH THE CRUSH

Don't laugh at 'crushes'. It's very common for youngsters to develop a crush on a celebrity and have posters plastered all over their walls. Your child may also develop a strong emotional attachment to a real friend, teacher or other adult and it's wrong to make fun of this.

758 LOVE IS IN THE AIR

Don't forget to talk about love with your child. Telling them you love them is a good start, but it's also a good idea to let them hear other members of the family talking about it and to discuss what love feels like with them. This is particularly important as they reach adolescence, when feelings may become complicated.

759 LOOSEN THE REINS GRADUALLY

Don't set your family rules in stone. If your child is constantly going on about how all their friends are allowed to stay up later or watch a particular TV programme, maybe it's time to rethink your rules. Discuss things with them openly.

760 MAKE THEM LAUGH

Instead of nagging your teenager to tidy up their stuff, use humour to communicate your point without making them feel defensive. For instance, say something like, 'How's the world record attempt going? You know, for the largest pile of dirty washing?'

761 BREAK DOWN THEIR DEFENCES

By the time your child is a teenager, they will probably react defensively to almost everything you say. Avoid putting their backs up by using phrases based around 'I' rather than 'you'. For instance, instead of 'you should…' say 'I'd really like you to…'

body matters

762 PERIOD GAINS

Studies have shown that women whose parents were open with them about menstruation when they were younger feel more confident with their womanhood as they get older, so talk to your daughter.

763 JOIN THE CLUB

If you're worried about your child being overweight, and no efforts to encourage activity and healthy eating seem to work, see if you can find a local slimming club designed for children of their age – being among peers is likely to help them to succeed.

764 SHARE YOUR CONCERNS

During adolescence, both boys and girls are concerned with the way their bodies are starting to change, what is and isn't normal. Let them know everyone has the same concerns at this time in their lives, and share concerns you had when you were their age.

765 FIGHT FAT TALK

It's not uncommon for young girls to start saying things like 'I'm too fat' or 'I need to lose weight' if they have heard other children saying it. Try to talk openly about weight issues, and make sure your daughter never hears you talking about yourself that way.

766 SEEK HELP

If you notice your child has cut down on eating and has lost a lot of weight, don't ignore it. Make sure you don't pile the pressure on to eat, as this could push them into secrecy. Seek professional help as soon as you can if you think it might be the start of an eating disorder.

767 GIVE THEM PRIVACY

Your teenager's body is changing in ways they could never expect and often these changes can happen incredibly fast and be a little alarming. Don't disturb them in the bathroom or tease them about looking in the mirror – it's normal for them to want to survey their new look in detail.

768 NAKED TRUTH

It's perfectly normal for your adolescent child to become self-conscious about nakedness, especially among adults of the opposite gender. Don't worry, and never force your child to show themselves if they don't want to. Instead, foster openness by not being too modest yourself.

769 BUY HIM A BOOK

Often, boys don't want to talk about what's happening with their bodies as they get older. If you feel your son wants to talk but doesn't know how, approach the matter gently by, for instance, buying him a book he can read and then discuss with you.

770 WEATHER THE STORM

If your daughter is the first to start her periods in her class, it can be a difficult time and she is likely to be teased by classmates, particularly the boys, if and when they find out. Remind her that the other girls will start soon and it's a perfectly natural part of growing up. Some girls worry if they haven't started their periods when their friends have; reassure them it's natural and doesn't mean anything.

771 HIT THE SPOT

Acne can be a horrible curse for a teenager, both physically in terms of pain and mentally because of the change in appearance. Speak to your doctor if you're worried, because there are now many forms of medication that can help.

772 OUT OF THE GRIND

It's common for teenagers to start grinding their teeth, especially at times of stress, such as before exams. Tooth grinding, or bruxism, can lead to permanent tooth and jaw damage, headaches and cracked fillings and enamel, so ask your dentist for a mouth guard.

773 GET A HANDLE ON GROWING

Teenagers – particularly boys – can experience growth spurts that can be quite a drain on their body and can leave them feeling uncoordinated for a few days or weeks as their nerves catch up with muscle growth. Don't worry that's it's something else, and reassure them that it's perfectly normal.

774 BODY CLOCK CHANGES

Researchers have shown that teenagers have slightly different body clocks to the rest of us, which means they are naturally programmed to stay up later, sleep longer and wake up later in the morning. Try to go with their natural rhythms as much as possible.

775 IT'S NO JOKE

If your teenager is excessively worried about their appearance, make sure nobody in the family makes jokes at their expense and remind them that other people rarely notice the details we notice in ourselves. Let them know about some of your own insecurities.

776 LET THEM EXPERIMENT

For a teenager, being able to express their identity, and experiment with it, is an essential part of learning who they are. Allow them some freedom to do this so that they can understand their own boundaries. Although you may want to draw a line at tattoos and piercings, you could allow a bit of license with make-up or fashion statements.

safety online

777 BE INTERNET AWARE

Be aware of how, when and where your child uses the internet. This will help you to spot any significant changes, such as your child spending much longer online than usual or using the internet only away from home. This may well be just typical adolescent behaviour but at least you'll be alert to the possibilities.

778 PREPARE FOR PORN

Talk to your child about the type of sites they may stumble across accidentally. You may find it an uncomfortable topic (and they almost certainly will) but experts say it's sensible to discuss the possibility they'll encounter pornographic material. They should feel more able to turn to you if things are getting out of hand and much less vulnerable to abusers urging them to keep secrets.

175

779 MAKE IT YOUR BUSINESS

Learn as much as possible about what your
child does online. Ask them to show you
the sites they visit and who they exchange
messages with. They may not reveal
everything but it's a good start and at least
they'll know you're interested. Make sure they
know the minimum ages for contributing to
social networking sites.

780 INSTAL SAFETY SOFTWARE

When first allowing your child to use the
internet, purchase software that will help
keep them safe. Your teenager does not
have to be looking for trouble to get into
it on the internet, and safety software will
give you peace of mind. Reassure them that
any site that is not dangerous can be put on
their 'allowed list'.

781 A NEW THEM

Remember some young people will use
chatrooms to 'reinvent' themselves, which is
perfectly normal. Use your intuition to work out
if your child's internet use is healthy and use the
opportunity to talk to them about related issues.

782 KEEP IT PUBLIC

To help keep your child safe online put the
computer in a family room. Show an interest
in what your child is doing on the internet
but try to keep a balance – not respecting
their privacy and intruding too much might
encourage them to be secretive.

783 GET TECHY

Many parents worry they won't be able to protect their children online because they are intimidated by technology, don't have access to the internet or haven't had the opportunity to learn. Try your local family centres, colleges, libraries and internet cafes, and ask your internet service provider for advice on protecting your family.

784 TAKE ADVICE

Talk to other parents about the rules they have for their children when it comes to internet use to double-check your child's safety. For instance, your child may know not to post a picture of themselves on a networking site, but that doesn't stop their friends posting group photos that include them.

785 MODERATION IS GOOD

Speak to your internet service provider about its policy on chatrooms. Are they moderated (monitored constantly) by fully trained adults to minimize the risk of bullying or abuse? It's never a good idea to allow children onto unmoderated sites.

786 HISTORY CLEARS MYSTERY

Check the history of sites your child has visited and make it clear to them that you'll do this regularly. If you are worried about them visiting inappropriate sites or if the history has been deleted, calmly ask for an explanation.

787 KEEP MUM

Explain to your child that they shouldn't give out personal information to people they meet on the internet. Stress that although they may think of them as friends, there's a risk (however small) that they're not who they say they are. Telling strangers their details could play into their hands and they should never post a photograph of themselves.

grades & results

788 CONSIDER THE CHANGE

Recognize that exams signify a new stage of life, and change can cause feelings of unease, regret and even depression. Be aware of how this period of their life might affect them and try to be considerate of their feelings.

779 JUST CELEBRATE

Mark the end of exams with a celebration, so that whatever result they get they know they have been valued and praised for having done their best. Let them choose their celebration, within reason.

780 PREPARE THE CANVAS

Encourage them to get pens and pencils ready the night before an exam and try to get them to go to bed at a reasonable time. On the day of the exam, make sure they are up in time for breakfast and have everything they need.

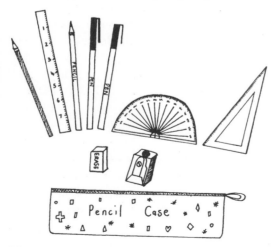

781 CUT SOME SLACK

If exams are coming up, help your child revise by rearranging the family's schedules and priorities. Go easy on them about chores and tidiness, give them a break and try to be patient with moodiness. If a child feels supported, they are likely to perform better.

782 SMALL AND OFTEN

Bribes or large presents conditional on getting high grades aren't the best way to help young people. It's far better to encourage them to work for their own satisfaction and schedule small and frequent rewards for effort.

783 PUT THINGS IN PERSPECTIVE

Reassure your child that your love and support is not contingent on exam grades. Everyone loses out at some time or other and failing an exam isn't the end of the world. They can resit, using what they have learned this time round to do better or decide to go a different route next time. Reassure and help them review all the options.

794 BE REALISTIC

Don't let unrealistic expectations of your children or hopes and fears for them become entangled with your own emotions. Try to separate what you might have wished for yourself at their age from their aspirations; support them in their dreams rather than pressurizing them to do it for you.

795 TABLE THEIR TIME

If your child is revising for exams, help them set a timetable that's practical. Work in time to do sport and activity, spend time with friends and also to relax and do nothing. Everyone works more effectively when they have the right balance.

796 RESULTS HOME OR AWAY

Discuss in advance with your child where they want to be when their exam results come out – at home or away on holiday (vacation). Look at all the pros and cons with them and if you can, go with their request (have an alternative arrangement in mind as well, in case they have a last-moment panic).

797 MOVE ON

Before exams tell your child you love and support them, whatever the result. Afterwards, let them voice their worries and expectations but also encourage them to let go and focus on the next exam or event.

798 SLEEP AID

Try not to let your child stay up late the night before an exam, even if they haven't finished all the work they were planning to do. Research has shown that late-night work rarely results in increased performance. They're better off getting a good night's sleep.

799 HAVE A PLAN B

Have a contingency plan for what to do if results aren't as good as you hoped. Reassure them that failing an exam doesn't make them a failure and that while you may all be disappointed in the results, you aren't disappointed in your child.

800 BROADEN THEIR HORIZONS

If your teenager is unsure about what career direction they want to go in, don't worry. Instead, help them make decisions that won't limit their future choices, so that they're still thinking about their future even if they're not sure quite what it's going to be yet.

801 FACE UP TO THINGS

It's not uncommon for children to have problems immediately after exams are over; this is often due to issues having been put on the backburner during the exam period. Now's the time to help your child to face matters that might have been simmering below the surface for some time.

sex, drugs & rock 'n' roll

802 ROLL UP A ROLE PLAY

Practise situations with your teenager so they will know how to react if faced with difficulties. For instance, try some role play in areas about which they might face tough decisions like taking drugs or having sex if they're not ready.

803 SEX, DRUGS & WASHING-UP

Try not to make talks about subjects that could be difficult, 'special'. Talk about sex, drugs or other issues as everyday things, while you're washing-up, walking the dog, tiding up and so on, to let your child know it's something they can approach you with at any time.

804 QUIT SMOKING

If you are worried about your child smoking, the number one piece of advice from the experts is to give up yourself (and ask any other adults in the house to do so). Children are much more likely to smoke if they see their parents doing it.

805 DON'T HAVE A DRUG PANIC

If you find out or suspect your teenager is using drugs, don't panic. Accusing, arguing or threatening won't help. Wait until a quiet time when you are sure they haven't used drugs or alcohol and say, 'I'm worried you might be using something. Will you tell me what's happening?'

806 DISCUSS THE DRUG ISSUE

Whether or not your child uses drugs depends on a range of factors like self-esteem, your own attitudes to drugs and alcohol and opportunities. Many teenagers use drink and drugs because they think everyone else is doing it. Discuss this and rehearse ways of resisting pressure.

807 SHOW SOME UNDERSTANDING

Children who are lonely or who are looking to soothe pain or anger they can't deal with themselves are more likely to turn to drink or drugs for comfort. Developing a good relationship with your kids and showing them understanding can help counteract this.

808 NOT NECESSARILY ADDICTED

Taking drugs allows teenagers to get high or shut out the real world, and many teenagers try something at some point, whether it's smoking dope or taking ecstasy. Drug addiction is much less common, so don't assume that because your teenager is using drugs they are necessarily addicted.

809 WAIT TILL THE MORNING

If your teenager comes home drunk or under the influence of drugs, there's no point trying to talk to them or reason with them while they are still under the influence. Talk to them the next morning. Try not to scream and shout but do remind them what appropriate behaviour is.

810 DIFFERENT VALUES

Try to accept your teenager will probably not have the same values as you when it comes to sex, but that such differences are an inevitable part of your child growing up into a healthy adult. Instead of worrying, try to encourage them to talk to you about their decisions in non-emotional, rational discussions.

811 PREGNANT PAUSE

If your daughter becomes pregnant or your son tells you his girlfriend might be, it is important that they get help in making choices about what to do next. Even if you are shocked and upset, try to be as calm, non-judgmental and supportive as possible, and let them know you are on their side.

812 DON'T BE SHY

Often, parents find it difficult to start a conversation about sex and relationships, especially to teenagers. Find out when sex and relationships are being taught at school, so you can ask your child what they thought of the lessons to open up the conversation.

813 BOTH BE AVAILABLE

Research shows that boys can become much more confident about their future relationships if they can talk to their dad as well as their mum, and the teen years is a good time for fathers to talk to their sons about the need to respect girls and to think about their responsibilities around contraception and safe sex. If mum or dad isn't available, another close adult will do.

814 TALK TO YOUR TEEN

If you are worried about your teen giving in to peer pressure or mixing with the wrong crowd, don't ignore it. Talk to them and let them know they can always use you as an excuse and you will back them up. Show them you understand the difficulties in standing up to peer pressure .

815 BE RISK AWARE

Talk to your teenagers about the risks of drinking and drugs when it comes to safe sex and how it's important in all situations. Try to bring it up casually, perhaps in relation to something you are watching on TV together.

816 LESSONS IN FIRST AID

Make sure your child – and preferably some of their friends – are well versed in first aid. Pay for them to take a course. You're much less likely to worry about them being out and about if you know they can cope with emergencies.

817 STALL FOR TIME

Make sure your teen knows how to deal with peer pressure situations by stalling. Let them know they don't need to give an immediate 'yes' or 'no' if they feel pressured. They can play for time by saying, 'maybe later' or 'I'll wait and see' if they don't feel comfortable.

818 CONSIDER THE CONSEQUENCE

Teenagers often don't consider consequences when it comes to their actions. Talk to them calmly and remind them that illegal behaviour could lead to arrest and even prison.

819 DON'T FORGET FEELINGS

As your child gets older, they may find it difficult to talk to you about issues like sex and relationships. Don't make the mistake of sticking to biology; it's often emotions they want to talk about. Let them know your thoughts and beliefs and encourage them to develop their own.

rights & responsibilities

820 HONEST TO GOODNESS

Encourage your child to be honest with you. If they're going off without you, you should know who they are with, where they will be and when to expect them back. They should always contact you if plans change.

821 CONTACT DETAILS

Even when leaving teenagers alone, make sure they know how to contact emergency services, where you are going and what time you'll be coming back. Teach them good habits by sticking to what you promise.

822 TRY TO BE REASONABLE

Getting teenagers to come home at a reasonable hour can be a major battle but it's important young people begin making judgements for themselves about safety. If rules are reasonable and explained (like knowing where they are), most teenagers cooperate. If this doesn't work, state a curfew and introduce sanctions if they're not met.

823 DISCUSS THE RULES

Let your teenager help you come up with two sets of routines and rules – one for schooldays and one for the weekend. Play the two off against each other (by adding privileges at the weekend if they agree to stricter weeks, for instance) and let them discuss what they think is fair.

824 BE SENSIBLE ABOUT TIDINESS

Untidiness is one of the most common battlegrounds between parents and teenagers – shoes on the hall floor, wet towels dumped in the bath, bags flung everywhere. Try to set sensible rules such as expecting your teenager to keep communal areas tidy but letting them do what they want in their own room (within reason).

DOOR MAT

825 OLD ENOUGH TO COPE

Most children aren't mature enough to cope with an emergency at home until they are about 13, so they shouldn't be left at home alone or to care for other children. However, all children are different so you should not leave them until you are sure that they will be safe and act responsibly. (Different countries have different laws on when children can be left without adult supervision, so do check.)

826 MAKE A PLAN

The teenage years – with competing demands from school, home, friends and extra-curricular activities – are a great time to help your child learn time management. Help them plan so they have a little time for everything.

827 ASK A POSITIVE QUESTION

Be positive when you ask your teenager for information about where they're going to be and you're more likely to get a positive response. Instead of saying, 'You're not going until I know where you're going to be', say 'Have a great time – have you left me a number in case there's an emergency?'

828 CREATE A WORK ENVIRONMENT

After a full day at school, the last thing your teenager wants to do is homework, so it's up to you to create a home environment that's conducive to them buckling down to it. Talk to them about whether they prefer quiet, music, their own space, the kitchen table, etc.

829 A CLEAN SWEEP

Experts suggest setting a rule that your teenager cleans their room or a communal space once a week, and they can start this from the age of 13. Vacuuming, dusting, taking out the rubbish (garbage) and tidying are all well within their grasp by that age.

830 CREATE SOME QUALITY

Most parents of school-age children now work, and most teenagers are just as time-starved as their parents. Make sure you find time in your calendars for a chunk of quality time with them – write it in the diary and spend it together doing what you both want, with no chores allowed. It could just mean going shopping together or having a meal.

831 FUTURE FINANCES

When your children are teenagers, you can involve them in plans for their future. Talk to them about financial investments, plans for further education and what arrangements you have in place in case of deaths in the family. Be sure to listen to their input too.

832 MOBILE BULLIES

Bullying isn't just about physical violence; today's technology makes it easy for bullies to harass their victims. If your child is a victim of text or prank call bullying, take it as seriously as if they were being physically bullied, and don't be afraid to change their phone.

833 STOP THIEF

To help your child keep their valuables – like phones and ipods – safe from theft when they're out of your sight, invest in some popper or combination-lock safety straps so they can attach them to their bag or belt. Neck and wrist straps can also help.

solving problems

834 GIVE AND TAKE

If your child's really upset about not having a new pair of trainers (sneakers) or some other object, is there a compromise? If they have a Saturday job you could offer to pay for half if they put in the rest. Or could you combine birthday and Christmas presents?

835 TEACH THEM THE VALUE OF MONEY

If you're paying your child for cleaning the car, washing windows, clearing out the attic, sorting photographs, etc, make sure they've done a proper job. If you don't feel it's up to scratch, negotiate a discount or give them a chance to redo it.

836 WHERE ARE THEY?

Older children usually like to hang out with their friends in public places, such as coffee shops, parks and shopping malls. While it is essential to give them the responsibility of handling their own free time, it is also important that you supervise your teen's activities; try to get to know their friends and find out where they go to hang out. Encourage them to meet at places and in neighbourhoods where their behaviour will be somewhat monitored by having adults around them.

837 STRESS REGRESSION

Some teenagers suffer regression at times of stress, such as increased clinginess and shyness. Keep an eye out for any unusual behaviour, especially during exam times, such as eating disturbances, nightmares and even sleep-walking. Other signs of stress include social withdrawal, accident-proneness, rebellion at home or school, aggression, risk-taking and abrupt shifts in relationships. Encourage them to talk to someone they trust, if not you, perhaps an aunt, uncle or someone outside the family.

838 HELP THEM SOLVE PROBLEMS

Help your teenager with their homework, not by doing it for them but by showing them how to solve problems. For instance, even if you don't know the answer to their maths assignments, you can help them research the answer by using books and the internet.

839 AGREE THE GOING RATE

Often parents will pay their teenagers for help around the home. Talk to them about what tasks they think they should be paid for and agree a rate beforehand – it's best to agree a rate for the job rather than by the hour, which will help them work faster!

840 KEEP IN TOUCH WITH TEACHERS

As your child's education progresses, make an effort to get in touch with their teachers – particularly if they have form (homeroom) teachers or tutors. Let the teacher know you are open to discussion about your child's education and wish to be approached about any issues that arise. Ask for the teacher's email address so you can correspond and reply at the least busy times of the day.

expanding the family

841 DON'T SPILL THE BEANS TOO EARLY

Time passes very slowly for children. Telling other children in the family too early about a new addition you're expecting will mean that they have to wait an awfully long time before their sibling's arrival.

842 KEEP THEM HAPPY

A new baby entering the house is hard enough for the parents, but it can be traumatizing for the existing child. Both parents need to make time to spend with the older child alone, so they don't feel pushed out.

843 READ THE MATERIAL

Reading books and watching TV programmes together about having a new baby can help your child come to terms with any changes that may be around the corner. Both boys and girls can enjoy having a doll to practise with too. Reassure your child that your love for them won't change.

844 HAVE ALTERNATIVES

If you're about to have your second or third child, make sure you've got solid plans in place for what happens to your other children when you go into labour. Have a plan B as well in case the first one falls through. It's important you don't have to worry about them when you're birthing.

845 USE REASSURANCE

Many small children are worried that the prospect of a new baby means they will be excluded. To combat this, make sure you talk to them before the baby arrives about all the things you're going to do together and how much they will be able to help you with things.

846 PROTECT THEM FROM PAIN

Your child will probably be very curious about the mechanism of birth of their younger sibling. Be honest but try to avoid telling them or letting them witness anything that might frighten them or cause them to worry about you.

847 PREPARE YOUR CHILD

Most families choose a two-year age gap between their children, and although this has its benefits, it can often lead to sibling rivalry. When there's two or three months to go, start preparing your child for the new arrival so that they aren't surprised by their sibling's appearance.

848 DON'T HOLD THE BABY

The first time your child sees you after the birth of their younger brother or sister, try not to let them arrive while you are holding the baby because it might make them feel replaced. Let them hold and kiss the baby but only if they want to. Answer their questions and give your first child lots of attention.

849 MAKE A FUSS OF THEM

The first time you see your older child or children after the birth of the new baby, make sure you give them lots of fuss and attention so they feel completely involved. Give them a present from the new baby and let them meet the baby in their own time – don't force things along.

850 A PLAY A DAY

Make a plan to give each of your children their own playtime every day. Even just 10 minutes of one-on-one playing can help your child feel more secure and build closer bonds. Let them decide what you will do and ensure all your children are given the same amount of time.

851 MEASURE YOUR ATTENTION

Often, the louder or more difficult child – this is commonly the younger sibling – will take attention away from their older brother or sister, but try to make sure the older child gets attention too, even if they're not clamouring for it.

852 SHARE THE LOVE

Try to avoid family 'splits'. One-to-one attention is important for all of your children, and if possible each child should get their fair share of attention from both parents or carers on a regular basis so they feel that there is equality within the family.

853 TAKE IT IN TURNS

If you are taking turns with your partner to put your children to bed, take turns as to who looks after which child, and try to divide your work so that each night one of you takes responsibility for each child. This will give the children more continuity and help them feel more secure.

854 STICK TO YOUR GUNS

Younger children often find it difficult to understand why older children have the things they don't and can do things they can't, such as staying up late. Don't give in – they need to understand that some things come with age and it's important for your older child to feel special as well.

855 AVOID RESENTMENT

If you are consistent and fair in your praise and recognition (and don't play the children off against each other), children are unlikely to resent praise given to their siblings. They may, in fact, be encouraged to offer praise themselves.

856 HELP THEM CARE

While you are in the first flush of love for your newborn, your other children may be a bit less certain. They are likely to enjoy the baby more if they play an important part in preparing and caring for them, and if you make time for them without the baby, as you did before.

857 A HOLE IN THE MIDDLE

While older children are often more responsible and younger children are the 'baby', a middle child has a less clear place in the family. They may feel left out and that they must compete for your attention. Make sure you spend quality time alone with your middle child to avoid this.

858 BEING OLDER BONUS

It's common for children to regress a little at the arrival of a new family member. Try to involve them in caring for the young baby, give them lots of praise when they are a 'big girl' or 'big boy' and don't reward younger behaviour. That way, they won't see value in being younger.

859 TIME WITH OTHER ADULTS

Don't allow yourself to feel a failure if your child seems to prefer spending time with other adults, such as grandparents, aunts and uncles or even friends – they still need you most. Instead, congratulate yourself on producing a confident child who's capable of forming relationships.

860 ATTEND TO YOUR DAUGHTER

Research into sibling rivalry has shown that older sisters of younger brothers often display more jealousy than other sibling combinations. Be sensitive to your daughter's needs and make sure she has her own quality time alone with you.

861 STAGGER BEDTIMES

If you've got more than one child, bedtime can be a difficult time. To ensure each child has their own one-on-one time, stagger the bedtimes so that the younger child goes to bed first, followed by the older.

862 INVOLVE THEM

Instead of ignoring your older child or using discipline techniques if they start acting up when you give the new baby attention, try to involve them in what you are doing and give them lots of attention and praise.

coping with twins

863 WRITE IT DOWN

If you've just given birth to twins, your pen and paper are about to become your best friend! With two babies to worry about (and double the sleepless nights) your poor brain won't have time to remember shopping lists or important details about food, medication, etc. Write it down to avoid mistakes.

864 GET OUT IN THE AIR

When you've got twins, even a stroll around the block can seem overwhelming but try to get out every day if you can. Simply walking in the fresh air has been shown to boost mood, and that goes for your babies as well.

865 PRIORITIZING IS KEY

For parents of twins and triplets, the first year can be completely exhausting. Time is your most important asset, so planning ahead is vital. If you're new to scheduling, try a traffic light system where high priority tasks are green, medium are amber and low are red.

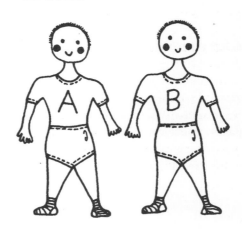

866 BE DOUBLE SAFE

Childproofing your home is even more important if you have twins. It is likely that you're not going to be able to be with both of them at the same time all of the time, so it will help you relax if you know they can't do themselves any major harm while at home.

867 ONE-ON-ONE TIME

If you've got family and friends nearby, try to arrange for them to babysit so you can have some quality time alone with each of your twins every week. Developing your own relationship with each of them will help them feel more independent.

868 JOIN A SUPPORT GROUP

If you're feeling overwhelmed by being responsible for your twins, join a group of other twin parents. Often, the parents of twins can feel isolated because parents who have only one child don't understand the pressures they are under, so talking to others in the same situation can help.

869 SET UP YOUR STATIONS

If you've got twins, popping upstairs to get a nappy (diaper), dummy (pacifier), packet of wipes, etc, can become a military operation. Try to set up 'baby areas' around the house where you can change nappies – one on each floor is essential.

870 DIVIDE YOUR NIGHTS

If twins aren't being exclusively breastfed, try dividing the nights between partners but make sure you do it so that each of you gets a good stretch of sleep. Do one night on, one night off or work in shifts – have one of you cover, say, 9pm to 2am and the other 2am to 7am (then alternate who does what time).

871 A WHOLE FAMILY

Parenting twins can seem like a never-ending feat but resist the temptation to always split responsibilities so one parent has each child. It's important for twins to see families as a unit, spending time together in the same way other children do.

juggling change

872 COPE WITH CONFLICT

Conflict between couples, divorce and separation can cause a lot of anxiety among children of any age, but particularly teenagers. Talk them through what is happening and listen to how they feel to keep their trust and help them deal with the change.

873 TAKE A STEP FORWARD

Step-families can be problematic in many respects, but discipline is usually the worst sticking point. Make sure both the biological and step-parent agree on a behaviour and back each other up solidly. Teenagers often take time to come around, but consistency should pay off in the end.

874 TRUST YOUR OWN JUDGEMENT

If you think your child is in need of professional help and you are at all uncomfortable with what is being offered or who is doing the offering, go on looking and talk to as many people as possible about it.

875 THE GIFT OF LOVE

Don't let yourself get angry if ex-partners buy the kids presents you can't afford. Remember all the things that you give them, like your time, love or simple but thoughtful presents that will be remembered long after the latest toy has been thrown away.

876 TALK ABOUT SPLITS

However hard it might be, try to talk to your child together about marriage problems, separation or divorce. Giving them the facts about what's happening and letting them know you both still love them and are there for them will help in dealing with the change.

877 EXPAND THEIR NETWORK

Some children like to have other trusted adults they can talk to – a grandparent, aunt or uncle, teacher or family friend – especially if there are troubles within the family. Don't feel threatened if they reach out to someone else; be pleased they are talking about their feelings.

878 HONESTY PAYS

Trying to hide conflict or separation doesn't protect them and may drive children away, convinced that parents lie and aren't to be trusted. However, balance your honesty with being appropriate – don't give them details that might cause them stress or try to assign blame.

879 BE UNDERSTANDING

Children who are going through changes, such as divorce or loss of a parent, may exhibit erratic behaviour for a while afterwards. Try to go easy on them if their behaviour is challenging, and encourage them to talk openly.

880 BEWARE OF LITTLE EARS

Even very young children are aware of and sensitive to conflict and bad feeling among their parents. Some argument is normal but try to avoid rows, shouting and sniping in front of them and if possible leave the house or remove them from conflict situations where they could overhear.

881 EXPRESS YOURSELF

If your family is going through change, members may feel differently about the same event. Try to let everyone express how they feel openly, and remember that feelings can change over time.

882 CIVIL CEREMONY

Marriage breakups are very difficult, with one or both parents often feeling hard done by. For the sake of your children, try to keep things civil – it will give them a valuable lesson in how to deal with conflict by cooperation and discussion. They need to see you both showing mutual respect to one another in order for them to treat each of you with respect.

883 TALK TO TEACHERS

Give your children's school some respect by informing them of events at home if there are difficulties – that way, they can cope with difficult behaviours and work with you to help your child get through problematic times.

on the move

884 STROLL AROUND

Keep your pushchair (stroller) with you in the airport – it's invaluable if your child gets tired so they can have a rest and you can keep an eye on them. You'll regret not having it with you if there are delays to your flight.

885 BOARD THE PLANE EARLY

When you're travelling with your kids, if possible ask to board the plane early so that you don't have to wrestle your kids in a crowded aisle. Then, wait until last before disembarking to avoid the crush.

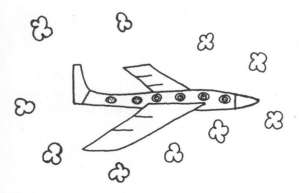

886 A TRAVELLING STORYTELLER

As your child gets older and their memory and language improve, they will start to be able to talk about their favourite stories. Travelling by car or train is a great way to do this – try to get them to retell the story or make up new stories for favourite characters together.

887 PLAY AN ALPHABET GAME

Play 'the witches cat...' with your older children to pass time on car journeys. Work your way through the alphabet choosing different adjectives, for instance, someone starts, 'the witches cat is an Angry cat,' the next person says '... Beautiful...' then, 'Caring...' and so on.

888 CHANGE IN A BAG

Make sure you take along a change of clothes in case of accidents, spillages or sickness. Even if your children are potty-trained, trips to the airport can overexcite them, especially if they're old enough to grasp the concept of the holiday (vacation) at the end of it.

889 PRE-ORDER A KID'S MEAL

If you're flying over a mealtime, see if you can pre-order children's meals through your airline or travel agent. That way, you'll probably ensure there is at least some of the meal your child will like.

890 TIRE THEM OUT

Think about trying to make your child tired before the flight so that they sit still. If you're flying in the afternoon, take them to the park in the morning or play a game of chase in the waiting lounge to wear them out.

891 TRAVEL OVERNIGHT

If your children are unsettled on car journeys, think about travelling at night or even early in the morning, so they stay asleep till their normal time and you get a few hours of driving in while they're quiet.

892 TAKE REGULAR BREAKS

Before you set off on your car journey, try to locate some possible stopping places where they can get out and run around. Picnic areas, parks and playgrounds are all favourites.

893 TAKE AN ACTIVITY BREAK

It's a good idea to take along a new toy or activity pack for your young child if you're going to ask them to spend a long time sitting on a coach, plane or train. Colouring books, sticker books and video games are all popular choices.

894 HOUSE OF CARDS

A great airport game for your pre-teens is to take along a pack of cards. They'll love creating their own games or playing simple ones like 'snap', as well as more complicated memory games. You could even buy them a book of card tricks or make a 'house of cards'.

895 CARRY-ON FILMS

If you have older children and have to make a lot of long journeys, consider investing in a portable DVD player to keep your kids entertained. This can also be useful for long flights.

896 DIG UP A DOODLE BOARD

To give your kids something to do in the car but avoid them getting crayons all over your upholstery, invest in a magnetic doodle board on which they can draw to their heart's content with no mess at all.

897 SING ALONG

Don't even think about setting off on a car journey with your child or children without singalong music. Let your child choose some of the songs or CDs, and let them listen to your choices as well to help pass the time.

898 DON'T STRESS ABOUT MESS

Long car journeys with children are not times to worry and fuss about mess. If you do this, everyone is likely to have a miserable time. Instead, accept the car will be trashed by the end and plan time to clear up afterwards.

899 KEEP A KIT

Keep an 'emergency' kit in your car so you're never caught short, even on short journeys. Include things like extra clothes, nappies (diapers), bottles, drinking cups, wipes, sunscreen, water and non-perishable snacks.

900 BE PREPARED

Keep a small first aid kit in your pushchair (stroller) to cope with those away-from-home medical emergencies. Things like adhesive strips, antiseptic wipes, tissues and bandages are good options.

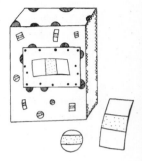

901 HAVE A SURPRISE UP YOUR SLEEVE

If you're on a long road journey with your kids, keep some surprises at the ready, like a new toy for each of them which you can produce just as they are starting to get bored. Make sure you choose one that demands concentration, though, to take up some time.

902 KEEP IT LOCAL

Often, it's easier to take children to less far-flung destinations on holiday where you won't have to deal with jet lag if there's a major time zone shift. If you do, allow them two or three days to adjust, especially if you've been travelling from east to west.

903 I SPY WITH MY LITTLE EYE

For little children, 'I spy' is a great car game. Make it more challenging for older kids by making it harder, for instance, '…that ends in G' or '…that has a double letter in the middle'.

904 CHECK THEIR BREATHING

Check on your child from time to time if they are sleeping in the car and don't have a reclining car seat. Studies have shown that their air supply could be affected in certain positions, so don't completely ignore them.

905 MAKE TIME IN YOUR SCHEDULE

Don't assume your children will go the whole way through a long journey, especially if time is of the essence and you're trying to be somewhere on time. Allow time in your schedule for plenty of extra stops and delays.

906 A STORY OR A SONG

To help long car journeys go more smoothly, invest in an audio book (many libraries also now lend these out) of their favourite story, nursery rhyme collection or songs. Sing along with them and encourage them to sing and do actions to pass the time.

907 GET A LIGHT STICK

Camping shops sell light sticks (designed for helping you navigate around a tent in the pitch darkness), which make brilliant diversions for keeping kids occupied (and helpful) if you're travelling at night. Or give them mini torches instead.

908 FOLLOW THE ROUTE

Don't underestimate the interest children have in maps. Give them a map when you set off on your journey and let them follow progress at their own level. If they become bored, you can use the map as a point of discussion.

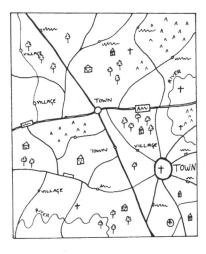

908 MAKE A MAP

For pre-schoolers in the car, why not give them some paper and let them create a map as you drive along? Tell them to draw pictures of some of the things they see along the way like trucks, buses, fields and houses.

910 SAFE COMFORT

Don't ever take your child out of their car seat to comfort them while the car is moving. If they are inconsolable, stop the car somewhere safe instead and get them out. It's dangerous to have children in the car without appropriate safety gear.

911 GAME ON A PLATE

Play a license or number plate game with your older children by taking the letters from a car number plate and making a phrase out of it. For instance, if the plate was AE54 SVB, they could make up 'African Elephants Smell Very Bad'.

912 CAREFUL COLOUR

If you're travelling to a friend or relative's house who doesn't have children and you're likely to have to spend time inside, why not buy your child a water-based colouring system – that way, they can 'paint' as much as they like without making any mess.

913 IT'S MAGNETIC

A great on-the-go travel toy is a baking sheet (make sure it's metal and not plastic-coated) and some magnetic letters and numbers. Let your children write messages and move the letters around.

914 TAKE TURNS TO TALK

Play an alphabet memory game with your kids – say, 'I went on holiday (vacation) and brought back an Apple', then have the next person say, '...an apple and a Ball', and so on through the alphabet.

915 SHOUT OUT LOUD

Play an alphabet animal game with your pre-schoolers to exercise their mind on journeys. Think of an animal that begins with a particular letter and get them to shout out answers. Whoever picks the right one gets to choose next.

parties

916 HIT THE PLAY BUTTON

Don't forget music at your children's party – it's a great way to help them get involved in planning and adds atmosphere to any party, even if children are shy and a bit quiet to start with.

917 HAPPY BIRTHDAYS

Birthdays signify maturity, so why not use them as a way to help your child understand the consequences of growing up? As well as their other treats, give them an envelope containing a 'privilege' – like their own door key – and an accompanying 'responsibility' – like communicating with you about outings – so they learn to associate freedom with responsibility.

918 EVERYONE'S A WINNER

If you're organizing a party for pre-schoolers, remember they like winning. That's why 'pass-the-parcel' is such a great game, because everyone gets a prize. Alternatively, plan enough games that everyone can be a winner.

919 THEME THE PARTY

If your child isn't sure what sort of party they want, it might be more fun if you give it a 'theme', like dinosaurs, football or colours like 'pink' or green'. Then make the food, games and activities fit the theme.

920 HUNGRY KIDS ARE CRANKY KIDS

To keep tummy rumbles at bay, have a stash of healthy finger food like fruit, cheese and breadsticks on hand. Limit chaos by seating younger children and bringing food and drinks to them and let older kids help themselves from a buffet table. Remember to buy more food than you think you'll need, especially if pre-teen or teenage boys are involved.

921 LIMIT THE INVITATIONS

Doubtless, once your child starts school they'll want to invite the whole class to their birthday party. Try to get them to limit it to a few friends, and if they are really resistant suggest they take in a cake or treats to school so the whole class can share in the celebration (make sure you ask permission first).

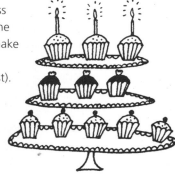

922 OUT TO LUNCH

If your older pre-teen wants to have a more sophisticated birthday celebration than the usual home party, why not let them take their friends to a café or restaurant for lunch? You and your partner or other parents can sit at another table to give them some privacy.

923 KEEP THINGS CALM

Avoid setting up groups of children in situations that could become dangerous. For instance, parties are times that lots of kids find overly exciting anyway, so avoid very physical games and loud noises in favour of more structured play, especially for under-fives. Make sure you have plenty of adults on hand to keep the children in control.

924 CHOOSE PARTIES CAREFULLY

Pre-teen parties can be fraught with problems. Let your child choose who they invite and think about basing it around an activity like swimming, ice-skating, ball games or even a picnic in the park, which will keep everyone occupied.

926 GO FOR FAVOURITES

Don't forget those old favourites when it comes to party games. If you've got enough space, 'it' or 'tag' is always a favourite, and it has the added advantage of tiring the kids out so they'll be calmer and hungry by the time you serve food.

927 PAINT SOME POTS

A great theme for a kids party is pottery painting – you don't have to go to a professional shop to do this, you can do it at home using clay flowerpots and poster paints. If you paint at the beginning, the pots will be dry by the end of the party and can be taken home instead of gift bags.

925 GOOD-ENOUGH BAGS

If your child's party has already emptied your pockets but now they're demanding goody bags for their friends to take home, they don't have to be expensive. A slice of cake, a few sweets (candy) and some photocopied colouring-in sheets is more than enough.

928 A REAL CARD

Why not make your child's next birthday party a card-making one? Kids love to involve themselves in crafts and on top of having fun making stationery, they'll be able to take their cards home instead of gift bags.

929 PAINT A WALL

Children don't usually mind bad weather, but if your outdoor party really has to move indoors because of bad weather, you'll still need activities to keep the children busy. Why not get them to paint a mural? Cover a wall (and the floor around it) with paper held up with masking tape and let them get creative.

930 HUNT SOME TREASURE

Why not set up a treasure hunt for the next birthday party? Rather than individually, get the kids to work in teams or as a group to solve your riddles, follow the map and find the treasure. Make sure it's not too long or covers too great an area as they will lose interest and may become diverted.

931 GET GARDENING

If your kid's got a summer birthday think about holding a garden party. Give each child their own pot and help them plant up a mini garden with flowers, herbs and other decorations. If it's raining, just take the pots inside and cover the floor. They can then take away a plant as their party gift.

932 DO SOME STARGAZING

Instead of going down the usual route for your children's sleepovers, why not get them interested in astronomy? Look for constellations and refer to astronomy maps – it's the perfect excuse for them to stay up after dark!

933 CHANGE THE RULES

Don't be afraid to change games to suit your children or to stop them getting bored. For instance, if your children grow bored of normal 'tag', play 'off ground', where anyone with their feet off the ground is safe.

934 SCREEN PARTY

Host a film party for your pre-teen, but don't let them spend all day in front of the screen. Help them with activities like making their own pizzas and popcorn or give them a film quiz so that when the film comes along they'll settle down.

935 CUT DOWN THE COMPETITION

Don't forget that pre-schoolers hate to lose, so try to limit the competition in your party games, especially if parents are leaving their children with you. Choose tombola or tails, and if prizes are essential for your games, try to engineer it so that everyone wins something.

936 POST YOUR INVITATIONS

To prevent hurt feelings, send party invitations by post rather than allowing your child to pass them out at school, or offer them by phone two weeks before the party. If you don't have a class phone list and your child's too young to gather details, ask his teacher for help.

937 TAKE PRECAUTIONS

Unless you want a complete disaster on your hands, avoid nap times and evenings for toddler and pre-schooler parties. Ask parents of children under three years of age to stay with their children, and make sure parents of older children leave contact details in case of an emergency.

938 SCATTER THE TOYS

When it comes to toddler parties, try to avoid too many structured games that will test their concentration skills to the limit. Instead, make lots of toys available and aim to create distinct areas for different activities so they can move around.

939 SAVE PRESENTS FOR LATER

For children under four, resist the temptation to let them open all their presents on the day of their party. Leaving some of them until the other kids have disappeared will limit the chaos (and damage) and provide welcome relief from the inevitable post-party blues.

940 ADULTS:KID RATIO

Parties with too many children and not enough adults are a recipe for disaster. Keep the guest list to a minimum and enlist other parents to help you, then offer to return the favour when their children's birthdays come around.

941 CHECK REFERENCES

Always check entertainers' credentials for your children's party. If possible, get personal recommendations from other parents or from the school so you can make sure the entertainment will be fun and appropriate.

942 ENCOURAGE IMAGINATION

As a general rule, children between four and seven will enjoy gifts that encourage imaginative play – stories, drawing and colouring. Choose puppets, dressing-up outfits and games or DVDs of their favourite characters.

943 OFFER A HELPING HAND

If your child has been invited to a birthday party and you're unsure about leaving them, or they're going through a difficult time, why not ask the host if they could do with a pair of extra hands – they may jump at the chance!

944 GIVE A NON-BIRTHDAY PRESENT

If your child is prone to jealousy, why not make 'non-birthday presents' a family tradition? Give the child who isn't celebrating a birthday an inexpensive present, like a colouring book and crayons or inflatable football, to help them feel included.

945 KEEP PARENTS INFORMED

Remember not to spring entertainment surprises on pre-schoolers, who might have strange phobias you know nothing about. Make sure parents are kept fully informed of what you're planning so they can raise potential problems beforehand.

946 TIME LIMITS

Don't aim for much more than 90 minutes for younger children because they are likely to be exhausted and become cranky. Pre-schoolers should be able to last a couple of hours, but try to limit the party to three hours or so however old your child is to avoid overexcitement.

947 SEND SIBLINGS AWAY

Siblings are often an issue at birthday parties. For older children, it's often best to get rid of their younger siblings (and make sure everyone else's younger siblings are banned too), while for younger children, older siblings can be enlisted as helpers. Alternatively, they could spend time with friends instead.

948 ARRIVE ON TIME

If your child has been invited to a birthday party, make sure you get them there on time and – even more importantly – pick them up on time too. It's inconsiderate to the party-giver to make them work around you when they are working to a schedule and have many children to think of.

949 GROWN-UP GIFTS

From the ages of seven to eleven, your pre-teen is likely to enjoy receiving gifts that make them feel 'grown up' such as watches and clothes as well as games and activities. Or let them choose their own present by giving them book, music or clothes vouchers, also a good idea for teenagers.

950 SEND A PERSONALIZED THANK YOU

For thank-you cards with a difference after your child's birthday party, take photos of each child at the party or a group shot of everyone, and send a personalized card containing the photo a few days later.

sun sense

951 LEAVE IT FOR 20

When you're putting sunscreen on your child, remember they should be covered for 20 minutes before you venture into the sun, and don't forget danger areas like the tops of ears, feet and hands, which are often exposed and frequently forgotten.

952 ONLY MAD DOGS

Tanned skin is damaged skin. Try to avoid taking your child into the midday sun, between 11am and 3pm, when the sun's rays are at their strongest and most harmful. This is a good time to retreat inside or under shade for lunch followed by a rest or sleep.

953 COVER IT UP

If you're planning to spend time outside in the summer, cover up as much of your child's skin as possible with closely-woven fabrics. The new UV-protective clothes for kids are equivalent to a factor 50 sunscreen.

954 GET A WIDE BRIM

Choose a hat that protects your baby's face, neck and ears. Those with peak caps and extra material to cover neck and shoulders are good, or wide-brimmed ones that cast a big shadow.

955 MONITOR EXPOSURE

When you're out and about, check your baby's skin and positioning regularly to make sure they are well-protected from possible burning. Adjust the cover on their pram or play area to ensure shade. Invest in a UV monitor if you're worried.

956 KEEP THEM COVERED

Remember that even in the shade, reflected UV radiation (from sand, snow or water) can still cause burning, so it's safest to keep your kids covered with suncream even if they are going to be in the shade.

957 PROTECT THEIR NECKS

A legionnaire-style hat or wide-brimmed hat that will protect their neck and the sides of their face from the sun is a good choice. They can even wear them in the sea or pool. Remember to still apply sunscreen as well.

958 SHADY CHARACTERS

Beach holidays and days-out are wonderful for children as they provide lots of opportunity for sand and water play, but make sure you provide adequate shade for them from the sun. This is particularly important in the middle of the day, when they can retreat under an umbrella or into a UV tent to eat and rest.

959 MAKE IT MINERAL

Many parents prefer to use mineral-based sunscreens on their children that provide a barrier against UV rays, rather than the combined or chemical versions that provide a chemical barrier that is absorbed by the skin. Most baby-specific sunscreens are mineral-based.

960 USE EXTRA PROTECTION

Glass reduces the transmission of most ultraviolet rays, but not all, therefore your baby will still need protection on long trips in the car. Avoid open windows that allow direct sunlight in and use window shades, blinds or tinting to provide extra protection.

bad behaviour

961 MAKE IT PUBLIC

If your child has developed a biting habit, don't hide yourself away. Many parents experience some aggressive behaviour at some point, so be honest with them about how your child behaves and what you're doing about it and they are unlikely to blame you.

962 USE GOOD BAD WORDS

Provide alternatives to swearing in the way you react to situations. Use common words like 'ouch', 'bother', 'darn', traditional phrases like 'fiddlesticks' and 'poppycock' or even make up your own alternatives.

963 KEEP A DIARY

If you're worried about your child's behaviour, keep a diary to see if you can uncover any triggers. Include what preceded the behaviour and what followed it and see if a pattern emerges. What are the pay-offs to your child? Are you giving the behaviour a lot of attention? Rather than worrying or blaming yourself, work at changing your responses.

964 SET STANDARDS

For older children, set the standard of language you will allow in your home and stick to it. Children over six should be capable of understanding house rules, so if your seven-year-old comes in using the F-word, you should sit down with them and explain why it's offensive.

965 DON'T LET WHINERS WIN

If your child whines and whinges, ignore it. Continue doing or saying what you were doing before. This will send the message that not only does whining not get them what they want, it doesn't bother you at all. If your child regularly resorts to a whining voice, make sure you're not encouraging it. Try to respond quickly if they call you and praise them if they don't whine.

966 MAKE THINGS EASIER

Try to structure your rules and routines around what your child needs, so you are setting the scene to help them exhibit desirable behaviours that you can then reward them for. For instance, if your nine-year-old is having problems with schoolwork, create a quiet place to work and schoolnight TV restrictions.

967 SUPERVISE BITERS

If your child has bitten other children, don't allow them to play unsupervised when it may happen again. This is unfair both on your child, who cannot yet control their impulses, and to potential victims.

968 BE AN ACTIVE IGNORER

If your child throws temper tantrums regularly and doesn't seem to be growing out of them, try a bit of 'active' ignoring – turning away from them and saying something like 'I can't hear you when you shout and scream' or 'I don't like that, so tell me when you're finished'.

969 TALK ABOUT ISSUES

If there are worrying things going on in the news that your child may have picked up on (like wars or abductions) make sure you give them a chance to discuss any fears or worries they may have and take them seriously, but don't prolong the discussion or you might feed the fear.

970 DOUBLE UP ON DISCIPLINE

If your pre-schooler is hitting, join forces with your partner to make sure they get the message that it is not acceptable. For instance, if they hit you, discipline them appropriately and then get your partner to reinforce the message.

celebrations & special days

971 GIVE IT AWAY

Instead of throwing away all those excess Halloween treats, give them to a charity or children's home. Many charities will accept food as long as it's wrapped, and it's a nice way to pass on a charity message to your kids.

972 A FAMILY BREAK

Try to take a family holiday (vacation) at least once a year where your immediate family can spend some time together away from home and not worry about work and responsibilities. If you're worried about money try camping, house-swapping or renting a mobile home.

973 BE ADAPTABLE

Parents often find it difficult to strike a balance between the needs of their child and other people, particularly when visiting friends or family who don't have children themselves. Explain your problems and meet friends in the middle – babies can be adaptable too.

974 CHANGE THE CLOCKS

Here's a sneaky trick parents can play on their children on New Year's Eve. Set the clocks two hours early and allow them to celebrate 'midnight' before going to bed. When they're fast asleep, move the clocks back to normal and prepare to enjoy your own celebration!

975 CELEBRATE YOUR CHILDREN

Try to make family get-togethers and traditions child-friendly. This is particularly important if you have the first child of the new generation, where occasions may not be geared to youth. Don't be afraid to change things to help your child have fun.

976 TAKE TIME OUT

It's easy to get bogged down in the responsibility of life, but it's important to take time out, too. Once a month, declare an 'at home holiday (vacation)' for your family when you take time out to be together, play board games, go on outings and share activities.

977 CHANGE TRADITIONS

When your family celebrates holidays or special events, allow your traditions to evolve according to what your children want as well. History is important, but if your children are going to enjoy family occasions it's important they feel involved. Ask for their input when planning food, decorations or rituals and try to incorporate their ideas.

978 DON'T BIN THE ROUTINE

Holidays and vacations are often a time when the rulebook goes out of the window, but be careful of abandoning the routine completely as a two-week break can be a long time for a child and they need routine to feel table and secure. Try to stick to the same meal and sleep times even if the other rules are relaxed.

979 KEEP THEIR HOME COMFORTS

Take some items from home to help your child feel comfortable while you're away. Things like comforters, toys, pillows and sheets that smell of home can help them settle into a strange bed.

childcare choices

980 DON'T SWAP THE CARER

From seven months onwards, babies usually begin to show signs of close attachment to one special person, usually their mother. This isn't a good time to introduce a new primary carer without sufficient time for the baby to get used to them (with their primary carer being present).

981 TRUST YOUR INSTINCTS

When it comes to deciding on appropriate childcare, trust both your instincts and your child's. If you or they feel uneasy about the person or place, spend more time looking around and don't feel embarrassed about asking lots of questions.

982 TALK TO OTHER PARENTS

If you're unsure about the nursery you've chosen for your child, ask them to put you in contact with some of the other parents. If they are reluctant to do this, think again about whether you want your child to be cared for there.

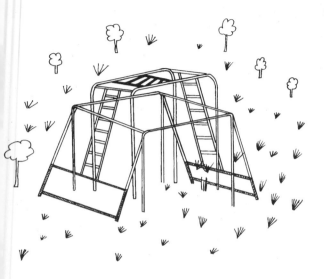

984 SHARE A NANNY

If you don't like the idea of group care but you're worried about the amount of money it would cost to have a nanny, think about asking an agency about a nanny-share. Many nannies are happy to look after two children at once and it halves the costs, so it's worth considering.

road safety

985 CROSS THE ROAD SAFELY

It's important to ensure your child develops good street sense. Your seven-year-old may still be holding your hand but soon they'll want more independence; learning good road-crossing behaviour could save their life.

983 SEEK OUTDOOR SPACE

If your child is going to be spending time with a childminder or at a nursery, find out if they will have access to outside space, outdoor play equipment and how long they will be able to spend outside – fresh air and exercise is important for mental and physical development.

986 TAKE THE EARLY ROAD TO SAFETY

The best way to instil a sense of road safety in your kids is to start them as young as possible. Explain what traffic is and how to behave near it, then involve them by asking them questions, such as where they think it's safest to cross.

987 BE A COPIED CAT

When it comes to road safety, always set a good example by using official crossings. Children copy their parents and it is estimated that three quarters of adults in Europe don't use a pedestrian crossing even when there's one available.

988 TEACH DRIVER SAFETY

A quarter of all 15-year-olds killed in road accidents are passengers in cars with an under-21 driver. Young drivers sometimes drive too fast, carry lots of passengers and drive under the influence of alcohol or drugs. Make sure your child knows not to get into a car with someone who drives irresponsibly.

989 FIRST-AID BASICS

From the age of seven, your child can attend basic first-aid courses that will help them learn how to react in emergency situations. These have also been shown to help children avoid potential danger, such as road accidents, by being more aware of what could happen.

980 CYCLING SAFETY

If your children are going to be cycling on public roads at any time, make sure they attend a cycling safety course. Many schools now run these courses, or speak to your local authority about available safety training.

981 KEEP THEIR LID ON

If your child is a cyclist, make sure they know to always wear their helmet and get their bike checked regularly for brakes, tyre pressure and so on, which could make a difference to safety. Check that their bike and helmet are the right size.

982 ON REFLECTION

Remember to put reflective strips on your child's clothing in winter so that they can be seen if they are on the pavement in the dark. A useful purchase are stick-on strips that can be used to light up bikes, bags, hats and so on.

bullying & abuse

983 REDUCE BULLYING

If your child is being bullied, let them know it's not their fault. Help them to act confidently, develop their own friends and spend less time on their own – all ways to help reduce bullying. Above all, let them know you support them.

994 THE RIGHT THING

If your child is being bullied and they've told you, make sure they know it was the right thing to do and you'll do whatever you can to make it stop. Let them know they should always talk to you and you'll be there to protect them.

995 KEEP A LOG

If your teenager is suffering bullying, make sure you keep a log so that when you confront someone about it, you have evidence. Phone logs, details of incidents and copies of emails or texts can all be useful to paint a realistic picture.

996 WORDS CAN HURT TOO

Don't accept that verbal abuse isn't bullying – it can be just as hurtful to a child as physical abuse, especially at vulnerable ages. If your child has seen fit to talk to you, it's obviously something they're worried about, so take their fears seriously.

997 BE A BELIEVER

If your child tells you they have been abused, it's important to believe them. It's incredibly rare for children to lie about abuse. Let them talk as much or as little as they want to and make it clear it isn't their fault. Make sure you ask your GP or social services for advice.

998 SPOT THE SIGNS

If your child begins to harm themselves, uses sexually explicit language or displays sexual behaviour inappropriate for their age, especially if they also seem withdrawn or fearful of adults or older children, it's possible they are being sexually bullied or abused. Talk to them first before seeking help.

999 DON'T BULLY THE BULLY

If your child is bullying others, make sure you talk to them rather than just scolding. Bullying is often a sign of low self-esteem, so helping them to address concerns or worries could help change their behaviour.

1000 INVOLVE THE SCHOOL

At the first sign that your child is being bullied, get the school involved. Speak to their teacher, help formulate an action plan and check regularly as to what steps are being taken to ensure that it doesn't happen again.

1001 CYBERBULLYING

Emotional bullying such as sending to Coventry or name-calling and tormenting, have been joined by methods like texting, sending cruel pictures by email or mobile. Emotional bullying can be hard to prove. If you find out others as well as your child are being bullied, you could get other parents together and discuss ways to stop it.

INDEX

Author
Acknowledgements
I would like to thank
everyone who's shared
their parental experiences
with me and especially
Frederick, for being my
favourite guinea pig.